636.6 Sutherland, Patricia
SU
   The pet bird
   handbook

DATE			
NOV. 1 3 1984	AP 6 '89	SEP 08 94	NO 20 '02
JAN 1 6 1985	JY 22 '88	FEB 2 1 '96	MY 18 '05
FEB 14 1985	SE 20 '88		
JE 16 '86	JA 25 '89	AUG 2 1 '96	JY 26 '06
	MR 28 '89	OCT 2 1 '96	JA 16 '07
JA 29 '87	FE 27 '90	FEB 2 4 '97	
AP 1 '87	MR 19 '91	JL 31 '9	
JE 20 '87	AG 26 '91	SEP 0 4 '9	
AG 3 '87	NO 29 '91	NOV 1 3 '9	
	AP 23 '93		
DE 30 '87	FEB 4 '90	FEB 0 1 '9	
MR 9 '88	FEB 21 '94	MR 08 '9	

© THE BAKER & TAYLOR CO.

THE PET BIRD HANDBOOK

PATRICIA SUTHERLAND

ARCO PUBLISHING, INC.
NEW YORK

Published by Arco Publishing, Inc.
215 Park Avenue South, New York, N.Y. 10003

Library of Congress Cataloging in Publication Data

Sutherland, Patricia.
    The pet bird handbook.

    Bibliography.
    Includes index.
    1. Cage-birds.   I.   Title.
SF461.S97   636.6′86   81-3441
ISBN 0-668-05279-1 (Cloth Edition) AACR2
ISBN 0-668-05282-1 (Paper Edition)

Printed in the United States of America

10   9   8   7   6   5   4   3   2

*In memory of my mother
and
for Abby*

Contents

Pablo, a Blue and Gold Macaw, stands on his head for owner/trainer, Glenn Cigala. Credit: Peter Sutherland.

Acknowledgments

No one learns a great deal about any subject except through research, observation, experience and help from other knowledgeable people. So it is with me. I am indebted to many well known authors of books and articles on birds who generously share their knowledge with others. I owe a great debt to the many birds in my past which gave me immeasurable pleasure in spite of my (I hope few) mistakes. I also want to acknowledge my long-time friend, Bill Saraniti of Brunswick, Ohio, who helped launch me into this fascinating hobby.

In particular, many experienced aviculturalists contributed to this book by reviewing the manuscript, providing helpful suggestions and encouragement, and generously allowing my husband, Peter, to photograph their birds. To these people I am sincerely grateful: Joseph Marssdorf of the Bronx, New York, a life-long breeder and exhibitor of canaries and other birds; Glenn Cigala of GC Productions (birds and animals for films), College Point, New York; Kathleen Pace and Patricia Kemmett, co-proprietors of Birds in Paradise, a bird store in Flushing, New York; Professor Carl Naether, who graciously answered my questions about pigeons and doves; Dr. Val Clear, who commented on an early draft of the manuscript and whom I want to single out with extra thanks; and Leslie B. Zeman, D.V.M., an impressively qualified and experienced avian medicine specialist associated with Cornell University at Ithaca, New York, who kindly agreed to review the book for medical accuracy and who answered my many questions.

I also want to thank my good friend, Robin Malki, who typed the first drafts of the manuscript.

Finally, I want to thank the photographers whose splendid pictures illustrate this book: Don Hunsaker II of El Cajon, California; Jean M. Hawthorne of San Diego, California, whose copyrighted photographs are reprinted by permission; and my husband, Peter Sutherland, who provided original photography and encouragement and who sacrificed so that I could write this book.

I heartily thank those who contributed to this book, and I relieve them of any responsibility for errors. In matters of opinion, those expressed are strictly my own.

Freep (cockatiel hen) kisses owner, Jean Hawthorne, while Rachet (male Mitred Conure) bows his head and waits to be scratched. Credit: Don Hunsaker II.

Introduction

Whether you plan to buy a pet bird or already own one, this book will help you care for it properly, tame it and train it, and, as a result, enable you to enjoy it. In this book, "tame" means your bird does not fear you (partially tame) *and* considers you to be its friend (completely tame). You will have trained your pet when the bird becomes manageable and when it learns specific lessons, e.g., to perform a trick, to speak, etc. Much of your bird's training (the manageability part) will occur simply as a *by-product* of your care and supervision. In other words, your bird will learn where it is allowed to fly and play, etc., because you have thoughtfully pre-planned its environment. Because taming success depends on having everything else in your bird's life right, proper care and feeding and housing and related equipment are also emphasized.

This Handbook also aims to teach you "bird sense" to help you tame and train your pet. "Bird sense" is just common sense as it pertains to birds. Take, for example, birds and sunshine. Common sense should tell you that an outdoor creature like a bird would probably enjoy sitting in the sunshine. So you might decide to set your bird's cage in a bright window. Bird sense tells you that an overdose of sunshine through glass is dangerous to your pet's health. A mynah bird placed in a sunny window would actually die! Weather permitting, you could open a window and allow your pet to soak up a little sunshine through a screen. Chapter 2 of this book is particularly devoted to developing this brand of common sense. But it is certainly not the last word on the subject.

The basics of bird taming and training are simple: proper management, "bird sense," routine and *patience*. Any bird, from a tiny finch to a large parrot, will become a happy, affectionate, disciplined pet if you provide the right conditions. A haphazard aproach will not work. Thoughtful planning, with your type of bird in mind, is necessary. After all, a happy and contented bird is a must if you expect it to develop the confidence necessary to abandon its natural fear of humans. In short, unhappy birds do not tame.

One of the requirements of the taming program described in this book is daily freedom. For any bird smaller than a full-sized parrot, this means flight space in a designated area. For large birds, freedom will entail daily removal from the confinement of the cage. Freedom to exercise and play is essential for any bird, whether or not it is tame. Later on in this book, you will learn how to provide freedom under manageable conditions. Within a week of providing freedom, you will regret ever having denied your pet and yourself this pleasure. It is really simple.

Unless you are willing to provide daily freedom, you will probably not succeed in taming your bird. A tame pet, after all, is a bird that will eagerly come to you with affection. A bird always trapped in its cage cannot come to you. I think an always-caged bird is basically a sad, miserable creature. The longer this situation goes on, moreover, the more dull and listless the bird will become, until it is finally a drudge to care for. So, if you are not committed to this responsibility, don't waste a bird's potential. Find it another home or consider another kind of pet.

This book does not assume that you have any prior knowledge of birds. It is to your advantage to read the book from start to finish because each chapter builds upon the previous one. The book is arranged to first introduce a large number of bird species from which you might want to select your pet. Basic bird behavior is then presented in Chapter 2. Feeding (Chapter 3) and general care (Chapter 4) are next discussed. Chapter 5 provides information on choosing the best housing and related equipment for your pet. Because this book cannot hope to cover every detail on the care and feeding of so many different birds, you are frequently urged to refer to the excellent books listed in the "Suggested Reading" section at the end of the book. The knowledge acquired from these other books will help speed your taming efforts, too. Chapters 6 through 9 are particularly devoted to the subject of taming your pet. Finally, Chapter 10 provides information on miscellaneous topics of interest to the pet bird owner.

CHAPTER 1

Choosing the Right Bird
For You

If you are thinking about getting a pet bird, this chapter will help you reach your ultimate decision by outlining many of the areas you need to consider. For example, do you really want a bird? If so, what kind? Where should you look for it? What factors should you consider when selecting your individual pet? How much should you pay? Necessarily, this chapter presents only a limited overview of the literally hundreds of bird species available as pets. For more details on a bird of interest to you, I urge you to refer to the excellent references listed at the end of this book.

DO YOU WANT A PET BIRD?

I often hear of the advantages of bird ownership in terms of "apartment-sized pets, pleasant songsters or amusing mimics, decorative additions to the household, an ideal companion for those who cannot have or do not want a dog or a cat." These things are all true. However, I sincerely hope that if your primary motive for obtaining a bird is to accent the decor of a room, you will seek it in a ceramics shop and not a petshop! Bird ownership, including tiny bird ownership, is as serious a responsibility as dog ownership. You must adequately feed, house and care for your pet bird; be its daily companion; provide veterinary care when needed; and provide for its care in your occasional absence. Further, you must provide this care for the life of the bird. Many small birds live from seven to ten years. Some varieties live from twenty-five to thirty years. Parrots sometimes outlive their owners and are passed on to the next generation. Getting a bird is not, or should not be, a casual decision. In my opinion, a small bird is no less of a pet than a St. Bernard dog!

Houdini, a normal green male budgie, flirts with his mirror image. Credit: Jean M. Hawthorne.

WHICH BIRD FOR YOU?

Assuming that you are prepared to shoulder the responsibility of keeping a pet bird, which will be repaid a hundredfold by the right bird, how do you go about selecting this creature? This is not an easy question to answer, as selecting a bird is a highly personal matter. Not only are there hundreds of species to consider, there is the question of personality to face once you narrow down your selection to a species or two. No two birds are identical; they are all individuals. Fortunately, like purebred dogs, there are similarities in temperament and general behavior within bird species. So you are not exactly in a roulette game when choosing the bird that's right for you.

In very basic terms, choosing this bird depends, among other personal criteria, on your budget, available space, and the amount of time you intend to devote to your pet. Different birds have different needs, so you should ascertain whether your budget, space and time will be adequate to fully accommodate your desired pet. For example, a large bird will generally require more space and demand more attention (and possess the vocal ability to ensure that it gets it!) than a canary or budgie.

Parrots, in particular, demand considerable attention. In this book, "parrot" means any large hookbill—macaws, cockatoos, etc. A tame parrot usually becomes as devoted as a pet dog, wanting to be petted and to follow you around frequently. The pet parrot, however, requires special treatment compared to a dog, and this fact makes the parrot sometimes more difficult to satisfy. You will have to provide frequent companionship under controlled conditions. Unless you are seriously committed to spending lots of time with your pet, a parrot is not for you. Also, if your *main interest* in a parrot is talking ability, *don't buy one!* You will quickly lose interest, and you and the bird will be ultimate losers. Making a parrot a tame pet should be your prime concern; teaching it to talk, secondary or even superfluous.

Broadly speaking, three groups of birds are available as household pets: hardbilled birds, hookbilled birds and softbilled birds. Each group includes a large variety of species with broadly similar eating habits and body characteristics. Only the commonly available varieties that are suitable as pets will be mentioned in this book.

A preliminary word about this threefold classification system may be in order. The categories—hardbill, hookbill and softbill—are useful to bird fanciers for convenience but are basically arbitrary. There is much overlapping in the characteristics these groupings are supposed to distinguish. In addition, beak hardness has little if any bearing on whether a bird is classed as a hardbill or a softbill. Would you rather be pecked by a canary (hardbill) or a toucan (softbill)? Rather, it is the *diet* of the bird that creates the most important distinction. That is, a hardbill mainly eats

Lories drink from a nectar feeder at the San Diego Zoo. Lories and Lorikeets are hookbills that eat a softbill diet. Credit: Jean M. Hawthorne.

"hard" foods (primarily seeds), while a softbill eats "soft" foods (primarily insects and fruit). An overwhelming majority of hookbills also eat "hard" foods, but the shape of the beak classes the group. Many hardbills and hookbills accept soft foods in their diets, but they are principally seed-eaters. To further confuse matters, there are some hookbills that eat only soft foods and some hardbills that eat just about anything. Rest assured that if a bird violates the norm of any of these groups, it will be spelled out for you within.

HARDBILLED BIRDS

The hardbilled group includes canaries and many species of finches, pigeons and doves. All hardbills are seed-eating birds (some foreign pigeons and doves consume a softbill diet) with pointed beaks and four toes, three in front and one in back. The well known canary is a perfect example. Male canaries and males of many species of finches also possess varying degrees of singing ability. Compared to the other families, hardbills, *generally speaking*, are more subdued in personality, less destructive, and limited in their natural inclination to learn amusing tricks. On the other hand, homing pigeons have been trained to perform a few life-saving feats. Hardbills are usually peaceful, gentle and quiet. There are, however, some exceptions.

If your motive for obtaining a bird is mostly to add a bit of nature to your household, look into this group. Just watching my canary zoom comfortably around my living room is a special thrill for me. I often marvel about our peaceful co-existence. And when he lands on the table to beg for a piece of an orange I'm eating, I simply feel very lucky to have such an unusual friend. Although hardbills as a group cannot really be described as playful, do not underestimate their potential as satisfying pets. My canary gives me as much pleasure as have many much larger birds in the past. And it was he who inspired this book.

Canaries. Most people carry a mental picture of a canary as a little yellow bird. However, canaries come in many colors, shapes and sizes. Beginning with the wild canary (*Serinus canarius*) hundreds of years ago, breeders have developed many breeds of domesticated birds. Today, canary culture is divided into three branches of interest: song, color and body type. Color breeders specialize in producing deep red-orange canaries (Red-Factors) as well as a host of new colors. Roller Canaries and American Singer Canaries are bred for song. Other breeders specialize in what are known as "type" birds. Some are bred for size (Yorkshires); others, for crests (Glosters); still others, for feather structure (Frills)—to name just a few. Type canaries and singing canaries are available in many colors and color combinations, including white, yellow, green, cinnamon, blue (gray) and brown.

All male canaries sing but there are significant differences in quality and quantity of song among breeds. Roller Canaries are bred for their special ability to sing a soft, continuous melody. Rollers sing with their beaks nearly closed, standing low on the perch. Other canaries sing a loud, rollicking, choppy series of notes. These free-singing birds are known as "choppers." They sing with their beaks wide open, standing high on the perch.

The American Singer possesses another distinct song. This bird was developed in the United States by crossing Rollers (for song) with Border Fancy Canaries (for beauty). Since Borders are choppers, the song of the American Singer is a blend of two voices. These birds sing more freely than Rollers and are more talented than choppers. When singing, they assume a middle posture. American Singers are also bred for body type but singing ability carries greater weight in judging these birds at shows. Available in many colors, this breed has become quite popular and makes an ideal pet.

Regardless of breed, all male canaries sing on a schedule that is dictated by changes in the seasons (changes in the amount of light and in the temperature). They should begin to sing in October and stop around June. December through March are the peak singing months. From June through September, the birds will be relatively silent. It is during these months that the birds normally molt.

All canaries are easily tamed, regardless of age, because by nature they are docile birds. Of course, it makes sense to buy a young bird. Advice on selecting one is offered later in this chapter.

Finches. One does not often hear of finches kept as single pets for perhaps two reasons. First, many finches are scarce (and therefore high-priced), so they are usually quickly snapped up by bird breeders. Very rarely does one see a single finch for sale; pairs are the general rule. Another reason is that some finches, like Zebras and the African waxbills, are hyperactive and simply too small to handle as pets. Also, in the case of Zebras, which you will find in large supply at low prices, they simply mature too fast. There is a case on record of a Zebra Finch laying eggs at six weeks of age! This is unusual, of course, but it illustrates the point. In general, you want to obtain your bird and tame it before it reaches sexual maturity. A breeder could hardly put a Zebra on the market that fast!

Finches do become tame, however, and there are quite a few species from which to choose. I recommend the larger varieties, like weavers and mannikins, because they are more suited to the taming method outlined in this book. It would be ludicrous to try to describe many finches in a few paragraphs. So, again, I refer you to the excellent books listed at the end of this Handbook. Simply as a guideline, I would suggest looking into Society Finches (also known as Bengalese Finches), Napoleon Weavers, Orange Weavers, Cutthroat Finches, Spice Finches, Green Singing Finches, Gray Singing Finches, Red Crested Cardinals (also called Brazilian Cardinals) and the birds that have to be seen to be believed, Gouldian Finches (or Lady Gould Finches).

If you decide to obtain a finch for a pet, try to determine whether the bird was captive-bred or caught wild. Your petshop dealer should know. Trying to tame a wild-caught adult, I think, is a little too much to ask of a bird. It takes time to settle down to life in a bird cage. It's simply better to wait for the next generation.

Pigeons and Doves.   Technically speaking, there is no scientific distinction between pigeons and doves. Doves are just small pigeons. No doubt, you've seen many "street" pigeons in your local park and have heard their characteristic cooing. Few have not seen White Doves (also called Sacred or Temple Doves) in a magician's act. Pigeons and doves are all intelligent birds, and many are easily tamed. Wild "street" pigeons in parks are tamed by the people who feed them. Imagine how simple it would be to tame the domestic varieties.

One fact you may not know is that pigeons and doves are the only birds of avicultural interest, except for Zebra Finches, that drink in a continuous stream. Other birds fill their beaks with water, then must lift

Two Fantailed Pigeons strut on a shady patio. These pigeons are often used as decoys to ground other domestic pigeons flying at liberty. Credit: Jean M. Hawthorne.

their heads to swallow it. Also, seed-eating pigeons and doves swallow their seeds whole. Other seed-eating birds first remove the seed husks.

There are about 400 varieties of domestic pigeons (utility, fancy and racing breeds) and another 100 or more species of wild, foreign pigeons and doves that are kept in captivity in the United States. (There is a world of difference between these birds and the common "street" pigeon. Do not let the poor reputation of the latter version dissuade you from pursuing the domestic types.) So, as in the case of finches, it is impossible to describe more than a few of the most common here. Again, I direct you to the "Suggested Reading" section of this book.

There are only three varieties of doves that are stocked with any regularity by petshops. They are the Ringneck Doves, White Doves and Diamond Doves, all usually inexpensive. White Doves are actually a white form of the Ringnecks resulting from inbreeding. The original Ringneck is gray, gray-brown and white, with a black band edged in white encircling the back of the neck. Many new color forms have been developed besides the whites. Diamond Doves are gray with little, sparkling white spots on the wings. Silver and fawn Diamond Doves are now available—again, a result of inbreeding. Diamond Doves are smaller than the usual dove (about 7½ inches long) and are peaceful with other birds, not other Diamond Doves. They are often kept in collections of finches.

All these popular doves are prolific breeders, so they are usually sold in pairs for that purpose. Elsewhere in this chapter, I emphasize the need to restrict yourself to *one* bird to achieve taming success. In the case of these domesticated doves, and domestic pigeons as well, you can drop this restriction. These birds are very docile subjects. Unfortunately (especially if you don't want them to), pairs of these doves will probably commandeer a feeding dish for a nest and proceed to lay eggs and raise chicks, almost always two per nest. Then you have the problem of housing the young separately and disposing of the offspring. Birds cannot go on breeding endlessly, so you might have to separate the pair eventually, too. Therefore, unless you are prepared to cope with the nesting activities of these birds, you should keep a single dove.

Being a lifelong big-city dweller, I have never seen a pigeon for sale in a petshop. Perhaps I visit the wrong shops. In any event, pigeon fanciers are *everywhere*, so if you want one, you will find plenty of sources from which to buy. If you live near a large, commercial airport, you can mail-order pairs of domestic pigeons (as well as wild, foreign pigeons and doves and other birds, too) directly from a breeder. See the pigeon-oriented periodicals listed in "Suggested Reading." These magazines feature many breeder ads.

Domestic pigeons have one extraordinary advantage shared uniformly by no other kind of bird—the homing instinct. Particularly with Racing Homers, but also with Rollers, Tipplers, and other varieties, you can

Australian Crested Pigeons share an outdoor flight with Ringneck Doves.
Credit: Jean M. Hawthorne.

provide your pet(s) liberty to exercise and forage outdoors, and it (they) will return. If you live in a rural or suburban area and there are no municipal laws restricting the release of your pet pigeon(s) in the area, consider these birds. The ability to keep a bird at liberty, I think, is the ultimate pet relationship. Of course, you will have to think twice about liberty if there is any danger of your bird regularly ingesting pesticides (as in a farming community), getting shot by hunters or killed by predators. To minimize the possibility that your pet might pair off with a wild pigeon, you would have to buy a young pair. This would heighten the birds' loyalty to their home. If you are interested in keeping pigeons at liberty, see "Suggested Reading" for information on how to go about it.

HOOKBILLED BIRDS

Hookbilled birds cover a broad range of parrot-like birds, from the tiny budgie to three-foot-long macaws. All parrot-like birds are seed-eaters (except Lories and Lorikeets) with hooked bills, thick tongues and four toes, two in front and two in back. Hookbills use their beaks and specially-adapted toe arrangement for climbing, using the beak as a third foot. This is good to know when your bird reaches for your finger or arm with its beak. It doesn't necessarily mean a bird bite! The parrot beak is also meant for "chewing," which is a favorite pastime. The larger the bird, the larger, more powerful, and potentially more destructive is its beak.

Hookbills are well known for the ability to mimic human sounds, so it is within this group that you'll find potential "talkers." Sex makes no difference in talking ability. Females are just as apt to talk as males. Although some species of hookbills enjoy better reputations for talking than others, ability is also a function of each individual bird. I know of a budgie, for example, whose vocabulary and propensity to talk far outstrips that of the most talented African Gray of my acquaintance. Joseph Marssdorf, who owns this talented budgie, Spotty, claims to have 800 to 900 feet of tape on which is recorded the bird's varied and incessant talking. I have not heard the tape, but I *have* heard the bird, so I believe it.

Noise-making abilities (including "talking" but especially the volume of sound) correspond pretty much to size of bird. So, if you are interested in a talking pet and are thinking about a large parrot, consider also its natural bird calls. Some varieties of hookbills (some of which are small for the volume they produce) are known for their ear-shattering screeching abilities. Wild screaming tends to diminish as these birds tame, but not necessarily in individual birds and never completely. The potential for screaming is ever-present. Many hookbills prefer the early morning to so express themselves. If you live in an apartment or an otherwise crowded neighborhood, you will need to consider this potential when selecting your pet.

Two Scarlet Macaws perch outdoors at the San Diego Zoo. Credit: Jean M. Hawthorne.

"Spotty" Marssdorf, male pied budgie (half-English, half-American), poses for a portrait. Spotty is a non-stop talker. Credit: Peter Sutherland.

The hookbilled group provides the bulk of birds people keep most often as pets. Therefore, proportionate to the hardbill and softbill families, I have devoted more space to these birds. Even so, I am ignoring whole genera of hookbills, including most Australian parakeets, Lories and Lorikeets, Indian parakeets, parrotlets and others. The information provided is necessarily superficial, meant merely to display popular birds and spark your curiosity to further reading.

Budgerigars. Affectionately known as "budgies," these are the birds most people know as "parakeets." The budgie, however, is just one species—the Shell Parakeet—of many species originating in Australia. Budgies have been bred for so many years that they are completely domesticated. They come in many exotic colors, all originating from the wild green and yellow bird. It is even possible to obtain a crested budgie.

The most widely available version of the budgie is the American-bred bird that everyone, no doubt, has seen. However, there is an English-bred type which is larger, not as high-strung and, to me, better looking than the American-bred pet stock. English birds are usually bred for exhibition at bird shows, so they are pedigreed. I think it is worth the extra dollars in cost to obtain an English-bred budgie. However, both English and American-bred budgies make excellent pets and possess talking ability, regardless of sex.

This budgie is twenty-four days old. Note the shell markings on the entire head. Credit: Jean M. Hawthorne.

It is best to select a young bird for quick taming success. Fortunately, a few obvious clues to age exist. On a very young budgie, the upper mandible (top half of the beak) is dark-colored in some color varieties; it will quickly fade to the adult, horn color. The normally colored young budgie's head is completely covered with shell markings. As the bird ages, these markings gradually, via the first molt, recede to the top of the head, about even with the eyes. The "forehead" then assumes either the typical white or yellow color. This occurs by about six months of age. The neck spots forming a necklace on the normal colored budgie gain better definition with age, too. Rare colored varieties of budgies, like the albinos (whites) and lutinos (yellows), do not have shell markings or spots, so you cannot estimate their ages as easily.

The cere (fleshy portion above the beak surrounding the nostrils) of the baby budgie is pink. In the normal colored male, the cere soon turns blue. The cere of the female budgie turns beige or tan and becomes brown when the bird is in breeding condition. The colors also deepen with age. The cere of a male rare colored budgie remains pink.

Lovebirds.   About the same size as the budgie, but without the long tail and with a heavier body, is the African lovebird. Lovebirds look very much like Amazon parrots in miniature. The Peachfaced Lovebird is the largest, feistiest and most often available variety. It is basically a green bird with a peach colored face and a rich, rose colored forehead. The beak is horn. The Peachfaced is also available in mutant forms. One is a pied form, where the green color is replaced in part or totally by yellow. Heavily pied birds are strikingly beautiful. Another recently established mutation is the Peachfaced Blue. In this form, the bird is basically a dusty blue with the same peach accents. The head color, however, never reaches the same intensity as the normal variety. Lately, I have seen advertisements for albino and lutino Peachfaced Lovebirds, although I have not yet seen any specimens. These birds would, of course, have red eyes. Sexes are alike in appearance in all versions of the Peachfaced.

Immature Peachfaced Lovebirds have grayish-green foreheads that turn to rose through the molt by about six months of age. A very young bird's beak is partly black. If you want a lovebird, buy it before the beak turns to the normal horn color; if so, you will have a much better chance at taming it.

Other popular varieties are the Black Masked Lovebird, the Blue Masked Lovebird and Fischer's Lovebirds. The Black Masked is slightly smaller than the Peachfaced and is also basically green. However, its head is black, the bill is bright coral, and it has a white eye ring. There is a little bit of orange color just below the black of the face on the chest.

The Blue Masked Lovebird is a mutation of the Black Masked Lovebird. Where the Black Masked is green, the Blue Masked is blue. The

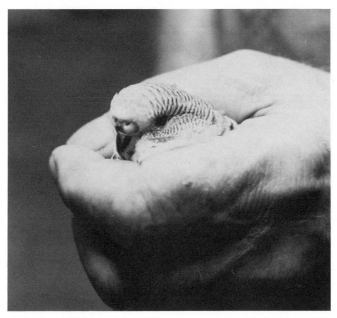

A blue budgie, a baby. Note the dark-colored beak and shell markings on the entire head. Dark color on an otherwise light beak is a sign of youth in lovebirds, too. Credit: Peter Sutherland.

Blue Masked also has a black head and a white eye ring. The beak is a light horn; and where the Black Masked has a hint of orange coloration, the Blue Masked has white. It is a real beauty.

Fischer's Lovebirds resemble Peachfaced Lovebirds, except that the bill is bright coral and the birds have a bare, white eye ring. The accent color is a pretty orange which extends to the bird's chest.

Lovebirds make excellent pets. However, they usually require more effort to tame than other birds of similar size. They are naturally fearless, approaching dogs and birds many times their size with complete abandon, and in the company of other birds, including other lovebirds, can be downright vicious. In fact, lovebirds are so mean that one must wonder why they're called "love" birds. I think it is because they huddle together on the perch, actually touching. Most other birds keep a social distance between them. One disadvantage to owning a lovebird is its shrill call note. I find the noise tolerable in tame pets, but unbearable otherwise.

Lovebirds are almost always offered for sale in pairs. Don't let their name or cute huddling activities fool you into thinking a single bird would be miserable. When they are not huddling together, they are usually tormenting each other. If you buy two lovebirds, you will not succeed in taming either of them. Either sex is amenable to taming, but a very young bird (right out of the nest, if possible) is necessary for best results. Believe me, lovebirds are worth the extra trouble it takes to tame them. They make engaging pets as they are extremely playful and talented.

Cockatiels. Next to canaries and budgies, the cockatiel is the most popular pet bird, and this popularity is well deserved. They are sweet and gentle, tame easily and become devoted pets. I recommend the cockatiel highly.

The original bird from Australia is gray with an orange cheek patch and a yellow crest. The flight feathers are accented by a band of white and the tail feathers are speckled with yellow. The female has a gray crest. Immature birds resemble females. If there is the slightest hint of yellow on the crest, the young bird is probably a male.

Several new color varieties have been bred from the "normal" gray. There is an albino, all yellow with the orange cheek patch and red eyes. There are pied birds, where some of the gray is replaced by white. Cinnamon and pearl-colored birds have been developed recently, too.

Conures. Conures are long-tailed birds, like parakeets, that resemble macaws. They are basically green with various color accents. There is a bare (unfeathered) facial area in each species, usually around the eyes. All conures are noisy birds and tend to screech. Conures are usually regarded as good aviary subjects, but, probably because of the high prices of parrots, are becoming more popular as caged pets.

The most popular variety is the Halfmoon Conure. It is a very pretty bird of several shades of green with an orange, crescent-shaped band across the forehead. The top of the head is a rich blue and the bird has the typical white eye ring. Immature birds have very little orange on the head.

The Halfmoon, I think, is a case where "popular" means low-priced and plentiful. I have owned three over the years and each resisted any and all efforts to tame it. However, three birds are a very small sample from which to generalize. I have read about many delightfully tame and talented Halfmoons, which is why, I suppose, I keep trying. My advice is to get a *very young* Halfmoon or none at all.

If you are interested in conures, also investigate the Nanday, Jenday, Sun, White-Eyed, Cherry-Headed and Mitred Conures. These birds are becoming more and more popular.

Small Parrots. Lesser known than most parrot types are a few varieties of small parrots which deserve more publicity. One of these is the *Pionus* family of parrots from South America, including the White-Crowned Parrot, the Blue-Headed Parrot and others. These are stocky, short-tailed parrots of about ten to eleven inches in length. The wings have a bronze hue, which is characteristic of these gentle birds. They are usually quiet,

Freep, a normal cockatiel hen, gives owner Jean Hawthorne a kiss. Credit:
Don Hunsaker II.

nearly tame from the start, and possess an admirably steady disposition. Rosemary Low comments that these birds are an avicultural rarity because a *Pionus* parrot can be tamed and will remain tame even when kept in the company of another member of its genus. I prefer these birds over any other kind of parrot. They make excellent pets.

Another family of small South American parrots are the Caiques. These are colorful parrots with the reputation of being playful clowns. Unfortunately, they can be rather noisy. The White Bellied and Black Headed Caiques are usually the only varieties of *Pionites* parrots available.

Senegal Parrots from Africa are stocky, short-tailed birds about nine inches long. Senegals have black bills and dark gray heads punctuated by yellow eyes. (Young specimens have gray eyes.) There are three varieties of Senegal Parrots, named for the color of the belly: yellow, scarlet and orange. Senegals are usually gentle and easy to tame. They are also quite inexpensive compared to most other parrots and conures.

Amazons.   Many varieties of Amazon parrots (about fifty!) are available and most make very good pets if acquired young. All Amazons are green with various color accents. They range in size from about nine to twenty-one inches in length. Amazons are usually slow-moving and sometimes downright inactive. This may be due to poor management, however, rather than a trait of an individual bird. Many varieties of Amazons are known to be noisy and somewhat moody in temperament. These drawbacks, however, have not prevented the Amazon parrot from becoming the mental image of the word "parrot."

The Yellow-Naped and Blue-Fronted Amazons are two of the group's better talkers. They are large birds and usually more expensive than their less talented cousins. Double Yellow-Head Parrots and Panama Parrots are good talkers, too.

African Gray Parrot.   The African Gray is reputed to be the world's best talking parrot. It is an alert, active and intelligent bird about thirteen inches in length. Young birds have gray eyes; older birds, straw colored eyes. Grays make excellent pets.

Macaws.   This family contains some of the largest, most brightly colored and massive-beaked parrots in the bird world. In spite of the size of some of these birds, they are usually very gentle and confiding as pets (if handled properly). They are highly intelligent and fair talkers; they also have incredibly loud and harsh voices. All macaws have long tails and bare facial areas.

The Scarlet (or Red and Yellow) Macaw is most often available. It is about three feet long. Almost as large is the Blue and Gold Macaw, another popular variety. Green-Winged, Military, Catalina (a hybrid of

Two Hyacinthine Macaws engage in mutual preening. Credit: Jean M. Hawthorne.

"Going my way?" wonders this Severe Macaw named Thomas. Credit: Jean M. Hawthorne.

the Scarlet and Blue and Gold) and Hyacinthine Macaws are increasingly available, too. All of the large macaws are expensive to buy and expensive to house.

For those who cannot accommodate the large size (or deal with the massive beaks) of these birds, macaws also come in "dwarf" versions. None of them is as strikingly colored as the giants noted above, but they are pretty in their own right. The beaks are still massive, however, by any standard. The "dwarfs" range from about fourteen to twenty inches in length and are basically dark green. Yellow Collared and Severe Macaws are usually available at reasonable prices. They make fine pets.

Cockatoos.   Surely, everyone has seen Fred, the talented bird co-star of the *Baretta* television series. Fred is a Triton Cockatoo and typical of the looks and personality of other white cockatoos originating from Australia and the islands of that part of the globe. There are about a dozen kinds of white cockatoos, three or four pink varieties, and a dozen or so black (or gray) varieties. With Fred as your introduction, you will want to rely on your homework for detail on these birds. Since they are all expensive, careful research is warranted.

In general, cockatoos are highly intelligent and long-lived. They range in length from about fourteen to twenty-nine inches. They are more prone to learn tricks than speech. Some are very noisy.

SOFTBILLED BIRDS

The softbilled family is large and diverse. It contains some of the most beautiful and oddly adapted birds known to aviculture. The tiny hummingbird, with its unique abilities to hover and fly backwards, and the large-billed toucan are members of this tribe of striking contrasts. Only a few softbills are discussed below; your research will introduce you to many, many more.

It is difficult to speak in generalities about such a heterogenous group, but there are some similarities. Most softbills, for instance, are highly active. The hummingbird puts in quite a day—sixteen hours—year-round! The pretty Pekin Robin is a good example of perpetual motion; it even eats on the run. Even the larger birds, like mynahs and toucans, seem reluctant to sit still for long. These birds are avid bathers, too. Another important similarity is diet. Although softbills display a wide range of dietary needs and preferences, none of them eats seeds.

The diets of softbills are usually too difficult for the average pet owner to supply; however, the advent of "mynah food" has changed this for many of them. Mynahs are "omnivores," the end of a chain of a somewhat loosely defined set of feeding requirements for softbills. The links of this chain include the nectivores, frugivores, insectivores and

A trio of Triton Cockatoos. While one is scratched, the others wait patiently for a turn. Credit: Jean M. Hawthorne.

Canaries (*left to right*: Red-Factor, green American Singer, cinnamon Border, yellow American Singer). Photo by Peter Sutherland.

Lady Gould Finch, male. Photo by Don Hunsaker II.

Ringneck Dove. Photo by Jean M. Hawthorne.

Budgerigars (*left*, normal green male; *right*, green harlequin male). Photo by Jean M. Hawthorne.

Cockatiel, normal gray hen. Photo by Jean M. Hawthorne.

Lovebirds (*left*, Peachfaced Blues; *right*, Black Masked). Photo by Peter Sutherland.

carnivores. The diet of the omnivore includes components of all the preceding (i.e., fruit, insects and meat), except nectar. So, mynah food can successfully satisfy the major dietary needs of many kinds of softbills. This food is available commercially, is as easy to feed as seeds, and helps to reduce the messiness of the birds' droppings.

Since the decision whether to keep a softbill often hinges on its dietary needs, the birds described in this section will be so grouped. All of these birds enjoy a good reputation for taming quickly.

Nectivores. If you have the means or desire to keep hummingbirds, pairs can be had for about the price of a parrot. It is better to keep at least two. However, some species will fight in groups, so prior research is mandatory.

All hummingbirds are New World birds. The ones you may legally keep in captivity* originate from the jungles of tropical South America, where foliage is abundant, humidity is high, temperatures do not fall below seventy degrees Fahrenheit and the sunlight lasts for sixteen hours daily. In captivity, these elements—foliage, humidity, heat and light— must be supplied and kept constant. So, only those who can provide the conservatory environment required by these little jewels should consider keeping them. If these requirements are met, the diet is relatively simple: nectar and fruit flies. Surprisingly, the birds are fearless, outgoing and easily tamed! However, hummingbirds are, obviously, not the type of pets that can sit on your finger or follow you around the house.

Nectivores and Frugivores. Another popular nectivore that also requires fruit and insects is the Yellow-Winged Sugarbird (or Yellow-Winged Honeycreeper). The male in nuptial plumage (feathers of the breeding season only) is bright turquoise and black with a black bill and bright red feet and legs. The undersides of the wings are a bright canary yellow; hence its name. The female is a drab combination of greens, grays and browns, with a black beak and pinkish-brown feet and legs. When the male is in eclipse plumage (not in breeding condition), he resembles the female, except that his legs remain a red color. Therefore, it is not difficult to distinguish the sexes at any time. A relative of this bird is the Purple Sugarbird (or Purple Honeycreeper), which is slightly smaller and has yellow feet and legs.

White-eyes are good cage subjects, too. Over eighty species are known (genus *Zosterops*) but only a few are available to bird keepers. They are small birds of about four inches, colored a pale olive-green,

---

* Federal law prohibits trapping or exporting for avicultural purposes all native birds. Birds that seasonally migrate to the United States are likewise protected by treaties.

with black feet, legs and beak. A prominent ring of white feathers surrounds each eye. The females are similar but slightly duller in color. A pair may be kept together and both birds will tame easily. The males sing a lively chirping song.

Insectivores. The most often available member of the group is the little Pekin Robin (also called Pekin Nightingale and Japanese Robin). It is a beautiful bird of about five to six inches that defies simple description. Its bill is bright coral, wings are gray and laced with bands of various colors, the chest is yellow turning to orange that extends on the underparts. The eyes are slashed with white and the rest of the bird is an olive color. Pekin Robins are extremely active, love to bathe, and sing a cheery song. They are easily tamed, too.

The Shama Thrush is another insectivore that is a superb songster. It also mimics the "song" of other birds as well as creaking doors and other harsh noises. This bird is about ten inches long, most of which is tail. It is basically black with chestnut underparts (like the North American Robin) and white rump and outer tail feathers. The Shama Thrush takes well to cage life and becomes tame quickly.

Many varieties of Tanagers also fall into this feeding group. These birds are small (five to seven inches), highly active and variously colored. All are pretty and most tame easily.

Carnivores. Birds in this feeding group are not often available and are really not pet material.

Omnivores. The Superb Spreo is one member of the glossy starling family that does not share the group's reputation for loudness. It is a suitable pet of about 7¼ inches from Africa. The color is a beautifully iridescent combination of greens, blues and black.

Also in the starling family is the famous mimic, the Greater Indian Hill Mynah. Greater Hill Mynahs (there are many varieties, differing basically in the pattern of the wattles) are shiny black with a band of white accenting the flight feathers. Feet, legs and wattles are yellow. The bill is bright orange. The Greater Indian Hill Mynah's wattles start beneath the eyes and nearly join at the back of the head. The wattles increase in length with age. The wattles of the Lesser Indian Hill Mynah also start beneath the eyes but curve upwards at the back of the head like a "W." The Lesser Hill Mynah has a poor pet reputation and should be avoided.

Toucans are sometimes available, too. The Toco Toucan is the most popular as a pet. It is very large—about twenty-two inches, almost nine of which is beak. The bird is basically black, with a white rump and orange and red accents. The enormous bill is orange with red and black markings. It is practically hollow and very fragile. Toucans are highly active.

Joe, a Greater Indian Hill Mynah, pursues his favorite activity with gusto. Bathing is the average softbill's greatest pleasure. Credit: Jean M. Hawthorne.

A NEW FAMILY: HANDFED BIRDS

There is one more "family" of birds from which to choose. The birds in this category come from all the previous groups, but especially the hook-billed group. These birds are *handfed*. A handfed bird is a chick that has been removed from its parents' nest before it is fully developed and is brooded, fed and finally weaned by its human foster parent. ("Chick" is a generic term meaning "baby bird." It does not pertain only to chicken chicks.) As a result of handfeeding, such birds lose all fear of humans. In fact, some of them seem to think they *are* human. Handfed birds are completely tame, even allowing bodily handling in many cases. Your efforts with such a bird would be simply to develop a pet relationship and train the bird.

Because of the time, expense and effort required by handfeeding, these birds command a higher price, but they are well worth it. Many bird breeders regularly handfeed cockatiels. Some handfeed lovebirds, conures, and Indian and Australian parakeets, too. A growing supply of parrots, including African Grays and a few varieties of Amazons, cockatoos and macaws are now available, too. Almost without exception, all Greater Indian Hill Mynahs are to some extent handfed. There are even a few breeders who handfeed finches, including Societies, Owls and Lady Goulds!

As handfeeding becomes more popular, more varieties of birds are becoming desirable pets. For example, birds that have not previously enjoyed a good pet reputation, like many conures, and birds that have tended to scare off potential owners due to their size, like macaws and some cockatoos, are now becoming widespread as handfed pets. Hand-feeding effectively destroys a bad reputation.

SELECTING YOUR INDIVIDUAL PET: WHAT TO LOOK FOR

Once you decide on a species of bird, you should look for a specimen that is young, healthy and blessed with a good disposition. Don't be tempted to buy pairs or "playmates"; a single bird is important for taming success. A tame pet usually reacts with jealousy and hostility to a "playmate" because it is forced to compete for food and your affection. Either sex of bird can be tamed, but in some species males are more attractive. Either sex can be taught to talk (if talking potential exists within the species), but singing abilities are usually male. If you want a singing canary, for example, make sure you purchase a male.

Your research will help you determine the age of a prospective pet. Typical clues to age are the color of the eyes, extent of feather coloration

This Jenday Conure named Jellybean is being handfed by the syringe method. Handfeeding is also done with a spoon. Credit: Jean M. Hawthorne.

and markings, and the condition of the feet and beak. Young birds have smooth, tender-looking legs and feet. Their beaks are usually smooth. In some cases, you will have to compare several specimens to recognize the differences between juveniles and adults.

Until recently, you could ascertain the age of a bird as well as the fact that it was captive-bred by its leg band. Many breeders apply seamless aluminum bands to the legs of chicks at an early age. These bands clearly and permanently identify the year of hatching, providing proof of the bird's age, and identify the bird's pedigree for the breeder. However, not all breeders band their birds. Just look into a cage of Zebra or Society Finches at your local petshop. You'll probably find that many are not banded, although every one was domestically raised. (Society Finches do not even exist in the wild, and Zebra Finches have not been available for importation from their native Australia for more than forty years—nor have any other Australian birds.) The point is, unfortunately, that the absence of a leg band does not necessarily mean a bird was wild-caught.

To further confuse the banding picture, the U.S. Department of Agriculture (USDA) has recently begun to band all birds that pass through its quarantine stations. Tiny birds are tatooed under a wing. Every bird that comes into this country legally spends time in one of these stations, where it is closely watched to detect disease harmful to native birds, particularly commercial poultry. At the time of this writing, USDA

The pin feathers are just beginning to sprout on this three-to-four-day-old budgie. Compare its size to the quarter in the lower right. In a few more days, it will be old enough to band. Credit: Jean M. Hawthorne.

bands are made of nylon and are designed to close on the leg like hand-cuffs. Unfortunately, many of these bands close farther than they are meant to, causing serious injury. As a result, a controversy is raging about the benefits of their use. I hope, by the time you read this, this issue will have been long ago resolved.

If you buy a bird from a breeder, you can simply ask the bird's age. Your petshop dealer should know the approximate ages of the birds in his stock, too. Make an effort to determine the age of the bird through conversation with the seller. Then confirm the estimate of age through visual inspection, according to the criteria obtained through your prior research. For example, if you are told a particular Double Yellow-Head Amazon is approximately two years old, look it over and compare it to what you have read. If the bird in question has a completely yellow head, including face and neck, the bird is probably much older than estimated. It is certainly no "chick"! Don't be afraid to take a book along with you when looking for your bird. You can then refresh your memory on important points right on the spot.

Health is equally as important as age. A sick bird might not live long enough to tame; it could also become untamable after recovery brought about by a possibly unpleasant treatment. It makes no sense what-ever to buy a sick bird. Even if you are offered a sick bird for free, it is not worth the other costs involved. So, pay very close attention to health.

In general, a healthy bird will look healthy and a sick bird will look sick. A healthy bird should be bright-eyed, alert, active, and in reasonably good feather. Keep in mind that Amazon parrots are not particularly active. Many parrots in petshops are not active because they really have nothing to do! Exposure to a constant stream of strangers will have them on guard, too. Again, rely on your research here.

Feather conditions can vary greatly. If a bird is crowded among other birds in a small cage, obviously its plumage will suffer. In this situation, there may also be a bully in the cage that has picked the feathers of its cagemates. In either of these cases, the bird's plumage will improve when you take it home and provide bathing opportunities and space to breathe. If you are shopping for a bird during the molting season (usually the summertime) the bird's plumage will not be perfect, either. (See Chapter 2 for more information on molting and feather plucking.) On the other hand, if you see a bird with naked areas where there should be feathers, the bird could be a hopeless feather-plucker. If you buy such a bird, you will be taking a risk as to whether it will stop plucking itself when housed in the ideal conditions you plan to provide. It might not.

A sick bird usually looks ill. It is likely to sit with its feathers all puffed up; its eyes will be dull or to some degree closed; its nostrils may be clogged or running, in which case the feathers above the beak will look wet; the feathers around the vent may be soiled, indicating the presence of diarrhea; the bird's feed may look untouched, suggesting a lack of appetite; and the bird will appear generally listless and tired out. If this description fits the only "Purple-Crested Tree Parrot" in town, and you've had your heart set on one, forget it and read on!

Choosing a bird on the basis of its disposition requires some experience with birds and a dose of intuition. If your petshop dealer specializes in tame or tamable birds, he will already have exercised his experience in choosing stock with good dispositions. While you're shopping, however, you will see a number of birds. Take this opportunity to observe how each acts as you approach its cage. Just by shopping you will get some notion of how different parrots, for example, react. Look for a bird somewhere in the middle ground—between one that cowers in fear of you and one that bolts to attack you.

SELECTING YOUR INDIVIDUAL PET: WHERE TO LOOK

Where you should look for your pet depends on the kind of bird you have in mind. If you want a handfed specimen or a just-fledged English budgie, lovebird or other domestically raised bird, it makes sense to start with a breeder. If you want a young parrot or mynah, try a bird store or petshop. If you want a hummingbird or a Red Crested Cardinal, try a dealer who imports birds directly.

No matter what kind of bird you want, you can get it from more sources than you may realize. As long as you live near a large commercial airport, you can buy a bird from a dealer located at any other shipping point in the United States. Thus, "the only 'Purple-Crested Tree Parrot' in town" argument is not really valid. However, when a bird is air-shipped to you, you must pay the ever-escalating freight charges. And you must rely totally on the dealer to select the bird for you.

The periodicals listed in the "Suggested Reading" section of this book provide many sources of birds in their advertising columns, including bird stores, private breeders and importers. Most of these periodicals also provide directories of bird fanciers' clubs. If you can't find the bird you want through an ad, write to the secretary of a nearby club, stating your needs. The secretary will pass on your request to breeders at a club meeting and someone will contact you. You may be surprised to find a source a few blocks away. Bird breeding is an extremely popular hobby!

When you're ready to purchase your pet, make sure you are dealing with a *reputable* pet dealer, be it a bird breeder, an "exclusively bird" store or a regular petshop. Today, more and more bird stores are opening up. Many of these stores are staffed by people who have turned their hobby of aviculture into a business. They usually know and care about their birds. Thus they are more likely to be interested in helping you

Freep, female Cockatiel, pauses from reading to preen her friend's hair. Credit: Jean M. Hawthorne.

choose a healthy, compatible bird for your mutual welfare than in merely making a sale. A good bird store will also provide a large selection of cages, play stations, bird feed and supplies, as well as helpful advice to get you started. I would be wary of a bird store, however, that offers only a few token supplies. Such a storekeeper is apparently not interested in what happens to your bird once you leave the store!

Steer clear of petshops with dirty cages, fouled bird feed and water and an unappealing atmosphere. Chances are good that such a store knows or cares very little about its birds. The quality of bird at such a store is probably low to begin with, and the longer the bird's stay there, the more likely it will become ill or weaken in stamina. I would also caution against buying a bird from the pet department of a discount store or department store, unless the shop has a good reputation or you feel that everything is just right. More often than not the birds are cared for by someone who worked in linens last week and hardware the week before.

If you have an opportunity to buy a second-hand bird, that is, a bird with a previous owner, pay very close attention to the bird's disposition. Birds are often subjected to mistreatment through the ignorance of their owners and can develop bad habits, such as biting, as a result. You do not want to obtain a badly handled bird as your first feathered pet. Unfortunately, bad handling occurs in petshops occasionally, too. I recently saw a bird-store clerk pick up a parrot by the neck—like a chicken carcass! I could barely believe my eyes. This fellow knows better, too, and the shop does a brisk business. Make sure the birds are treated with respect when you're visiting the stores.

A warning is in order about buying a bird of unknown origin. Millions of dollars are spent every year by the federal government to stop the illegal importation of birds into this country. But the score is not too good, as many birds are smuggled in. Buying a bird that has not been screened through the USDA quarantine system involves a tremendous risk. A problem bird could endanger thousands of native and pet birds, not to mention your own health. Buying a bird from the back of a truck or other fly-by-night or hole-in-the-wall operation is extremely unwise. If the price is suspiciously low, ask yourself why.

HOW MUCH SHOULD YOU PAY?

The prices of birds are determined in the same way as the prices of other goods and services in the marketplace. Domestically raised birds, like budgies, canaries, lovebirds and so forth, breed freely; therefore, they are relatively abundant. The prices of these birds are lower on the average than those charged for birds that breed infrequently or have to be imported. Rare mutations are worth more than the original types for the same reason.

Fancy color varieties—for example, albino cockatiels, violet budgies and pied lovebirds—are always more expensive than the original colors. But, in terms of pet potential and satisfaction, there is no difference between a male albino cockatiel and a female gray cockatiel—except the price! Handfed birds are always more expensive than conventionally raised birds. In species where bright colors or singing abilities are restricted to males, the females of the species are usually less expensive, if they are available at all. Occasionally, however, the females are more expensive. It depends on the type of bird. In the parrot world, birds that have excellent reputations for talking ability are usually more expensive than those that haven't.

For each kind of bird, there is usually a range of prices at which the bird can be bought. For example, if you want a green budgie you can get a "dimestore" bird for half (or less) the price of a pedigreed English-bred bird. The American-bred budgie you get in the dimestore is cheap because it has been mass-produced. It is more likely to be of inferior stamina (perhaps from overbred stock) and to carry mites or similar pests. In budgies, and similar birds, you generally get what you pay for.

The best advice I can offer is to shop around for your bird and compare prices and quality. Buying the cheapest bird is not necessarily the wisest action. As I've heard time and time again, "It costs the same to feed a good bird as it does to feed a bad one."

CHAPTER 2

Bird Behavior

Understanding basic bird behavior is one of the best ways to develop "bird sense"—a special brand of the more common "common sense." Knowing what makes our feathered friends tick is essential to taming and proper handling. This chapter provides a general guide to typical caged bird behavior as well as suggestions on how to use this knowledge to aid your taming and training efforts. The discussion is roughly divided into everyday habits and lifelong cycles.

EATING

In captivity, all birds are fed a staple diet and clean, fresh water. This diet is supplemented by vitamins and minerals and extras, like leafy greens, vegetables, fruit, nuts, insects and special seeds. The extras, although necessary to varying degrees according to species of bird, are definite "goodies" to your bird. Doling out the "goodies" in a thoughtful way will aid your taming efforts tremendously, as you'll see later.

Birds eat during daylight only, so your bird should be located in a bright room where it will have maximum eating opportunities. In the normal caged bird situation, I feel that food should be available to the bird constantly. Many birds eat small quantities at frequent intervals.

There are some who would quarrel with this feeding method, however, asserting that caged pets become picky and wasteful in their eating habits. Indeed, some parrots develop the exasperating habit of cracking seeds open just for the fun of it. Since they usually won't eat a hulled seed, it is wasted. These people advocate feeding the bird twice a day, once in the early morning and again in the late afternoon. There is nothing wrong with this feeding schedule as long as you can stick to it. Many pigeon breeders routinely feed their flocks twice a day with no harm to the birds. In fact, it helps to tame and keep them tame. That is, the birds become attuned to their keeper quickly, realizing who is providing the food.

34

Rachet, a Mitred Conure, takes a splashy bath in a Pyrex dish. Credit: Jean M. Hawthorne.

For most pet situations, though, it is simply easier to provide a dish of feed and leave it before the bird until it is time to refill. This option does *not* include water, which should be available at all times.

BATHING AND GROOMING

In the wild, birds bathe according to the opportunities presented by their habitats. Birds that spend most of their lives high in the treetops, like some species of parrots, depend on rainfall for bathing. In captivity, they tend to appreciate a sprinkle or spray bath. Others, like the popular budgie, walk through wet grasses, and still others will splash in puddles or water shores. These birds usually take to a pan-of-water bath.

Besides being a necessary activity, bathing seems to delight most birds. If you provide frequent bathing opportunities for your bird, especially during its free period, it will serve as a taming and management aid. After all, a bath is just another "goodie" provided by you. Also, a just-bathed bird will be easier to return to its cage because a wet bird cannot fly nearly as well as a dry one.

However, bathing doesn't come naturally to every bird. Captivity seems to stifle this natural instinct. If your bird doesn't accept a bath at first, keep trying. If necessary, change bathtubs or methods—for example, spraying, sprinkling, pan of water, or combinations. If you persist, your bird will eventually learn to bathe and find out it's fun. Your bird will look and feel better, too.

Preening. Especially after a bath, but also at any other time during its daily routine, your bird will spend hours preening its feathers. Preening, to a bird, is something like hair-brushing to a human. A bird will take each feather, one at a time, in its beak and groom it. The purpose of this, however, is not especially for good looks but to maintain the feathers' waterproofing.

Most birds have an oil gland located near the base of the tail. The oil from this gland is spread by the beak over each feather, from quill to tip. A few varieties of hookbills do not have oil glands for grooming and waterproofing. Instead, the tips of their downy feathers disintegrate gradually and provide a powdery substance which serves the waterproofing purpose—like baby powder! Cockatiels and many cockatoos are examples of this type of bird. If you see this, you will now know it is not bird dandruff. Preening is fun for your bird. Many birds preen each other as a show of friendship. A tame pet will probably preen your hair, and your eyebrows if you allow it.

Preening is a natural grooming instinct. It does not indicate the presence of mites, lice or other pests. The presence of pests would be signalled by intense scratching. Your bird, of course, deserves protection

Budgie, Houdini, reaches toward his oil gland while preening his feathers.
Credit: Jean M. Hawthorne.

from these pests, but don't go overboard with a single bird. If you suspect your bird has external parasites, see Chapter 4 for more information.

Feather-Plucking.   Preening sometimes turns to habitual feather-plucking with some pet birds. These individuals persistently denude themselves in what must be a heavy drain of energy and vitality. Feather quills are charged with blood, so constant replacement of picked feathers puts extra stress on the bird's system. In serious cases, the feathers eventually stop growing back, resulting in a permanently naked—and unsightly—bird. No one seems to know exactly what triggers this distressing habit, but boredom and diet deficiences are likely to be the causes. If you feed your pet a balanced diet and provide plenty of diversions and companionship, you will never see this horrible habit. Prevention is the best cure.

MOBILITY

A bird's body is designed for flight; its very existence depends on it. A wild bird flies to find food and shelter as well as to escape predators. In captivity, a bird does not adapt its body design; it needs to fly just to keep in shape. You should, therefore, make every effort to satisfy your pet's basic need for exercise, via its housing and freedom to use fly-and-play facilities.

Since birds generally fly toward light, you can discourage your bird from entering off-limit areas simply by darkening these rooms (that is, if you can't just shut doors). This is the principle used by modern zoos to contain birds. They do not use cages; they make the people-area dark, the planted area for birds well lighted. The result of this simple system is that the birds stay where they belong and very seldom is a bird lost.

When grounded, most little birds "hop," while larger birds walk. The larger the bird, the more likely it is that the walk will turn into a comical "waddle." Hookbills are feathered monkeys. Using the beak, they can climb cage wires, chains, drapery or pant legs. One of their favorite positions is hanging upside down by one foot.

FEARS AND PREFERENCES

The first fear you will have to deal with is your bird's natural fear of humans. This is the fear you must eliminate by your *consistent* gentleness, kindness and consideration when dealing with your pet. This fear will become crystal-clear when you observe the behavior of your newly-acquired, untamed pet as well as the first time you put your hand into the bird's cage. The bird will be shaken from the experience of being caught, manhandled, put in a box and jiggled on its way "home." When you finally release the bird into its cage, it may be too frightened to use a perch. Very likely, it will eat very little—and nothing at all if you watch it, for the first full day. When you reach into the cage, the bird will try to get as far away from you as possible, as soon as possible. Until you win the bird's confidence, it will regard you as a formidable giant. This is why scarecrows work!

In nature, birds are not fighters. However, a trapped bird, which is exactly what a caged bird is, will make every attempt to scare you away. The bigger the bird, the bigger is its show of bravado. A cockatiel will hiss like a snake. A parrot will ruffle its feathers and may even swipe at you with its beak, without making contact. Unless your bird is *extremely* frightened, in 99.9 percent of all cases, this is *all* show. Understand this. It will disappear as you gain the bird's confidence. So, don't be overly aggressive with your untamed pet—except to show it kindness.

I remember once seeing a demonstration of the reaction of a baby duckling to a great shadow overhead. This duck had been hatched indoors and had never been in an outdoor environment. When the duck perceived the shadow, it instinctively reacted as if it were in danger, as though a predator were swooping overhead. A caged bird has much the same re-action, for the same reasons, when approached from behind or above. The bird will either hear you coming or perceive the shadow, so it serves no purpose to approach it this way. In general, it is impossible to sneak up on a bird anyway, because the bird's field of vision is much greater than ours. If you can see the bird's eye, the bird can see you.

Chasing your bird is the next worst step. If there was any doubt about your intentions in the bird's mind, chasing will confirm its wildest fears. So, don't do this *ever*. Chasing will undo all your progress and produce a frenzied bird. For the few times you will have to retrieve your pet before it is tamed, approach it from the front and avoid swooping down on it. You will learn several safe retrieval methods in the following chapters.

Invariably, a bird prefers being *high* rather than low. This simple concept will prove invaluable many times when you want to retrieve or manage your pet. In captivity a bird will always sleep on the highest available perch where it feels safest. (If it doesn't, take it as a sign of illness.) In this same vein, birds prefer to step *up* rather than in any other direction. When you offer your bird a perch, be it wooden or flesh, place it just higher than its feet.

Birds hate to be handled bodily. Only the tamest of birds sometimes allow this. Therefore, keep physical handling to an absolute minimum. Especially if the bird is not yet tamed, if possible have your veterinarian or petshop dealer perform the few operations requiring bodily restraint, such as toenail trimming, wing-clipping and administration of medicine. It is better not to do anything nasty to the bird yourself. Have a stranger (to the bird) do it. Indiscriminate handling will otherwise result in a biting bird.

Don't neglect your bird's health or safety, however, for fear of its

The dark lines through the bare facial area of this Severe Macaw are tiny
feathers. Note the thick tongue. Credit: Jean M. Hawthorne.

reaction to being handled by you. If you must handle the bird, use an intermediate object, like a towel or gloves. The bird mentality seems usually to blame the intermediate object rather than you for its discomfort and distress. That this is true is evidenced by the large number of pet birds that show great fear of gloves! I once owned a bird that was terrified of towels.

BITING

As previously mentioned, parrot-like birds use their hooked bills like a third foot to grasp and climb. If you offer your parrot-like bird your finger or arm as a perch, it may quite naturally reach for you with its beak. If it is one of the bird's first attempts, it will be taking a risk and will approach you timidly. Don't be afraid of a bite and hastily withdraw! Your brave pet is simply grasping and testing the strength or stability of the perch. If you need more assurance with your parrot, present a closed fist when you offer your hand or arm. The bird will then not be able to get a good beakhold on your fingers.

During your taming effort it is reasonable to expect a certain amount of "curiosity" nibbling, whether your pet was handfed or not. This might (or might not at all) occur when you make your first physical contacts with your new pet, probably when offering food directly from your hand. For example, if you hold a wedge of apple for your canary, the bird will peck at the apple and maybe once or twice at your fingers. The bird wants to know what you're made of—even to know if you're edible! This is painless, harmless curiosity. You will realize this as you gradually get to know your little pet and see its confidence in you growing.

Unfortunately, the same harmless curiosity in a larger bird might not seem so painless! I once had to pry open the beak of a curious, handfed Amazon to release my finger from its vise-grip. How do you deal with this? With understanding and *composure*. If the large bird nibbles at all, the first nibble will probably be a gentle grasping of your finger. It will feel just as if *you* had taken hold of your own finger with your other hand. The bird may squeeze harder with its next try. As long as the bird is squeezing, you may feel uncomfortable, but this is not painful. In fact, this doesn't even qualify as a "bite." Remember that birds, like dogs, do not have hands, so they are beak- or mouth-oriented.

Your pet has a right to get to know you, too. Try not to pull away from your parrot in fear. If the bird's curiosity overwhelms you, simply say, "No!" or, "Don't bite!" When your pet gets to know you, you will be amazed at the gentleness with which it will use its beak to hold your finger, nibble your cheek, preen your hair or kiss you. You will never know this gentleness unless you are willing to take a risk in the beginning of your relationship. Just think of how big you are in your pet's eyes and how much bravery you expect from the bird. Until you get to know your bird and its disposition, you will be wise to view its beak with respect, but foolish to view it with fear and hesitation.

The only form of "biting" that should not be tolerated is a bite that actually draws blood. Fortunately, this seldom happens because it's easily avoided. (If it happens to you, you will learn that it's not so terrible an experience anyway.) Bird bites can be avoided simply by not frightening the bird. *An untamed bird will bite only as a last resort, out of fear.* So, if you don't push your bird into such a situation, you will never know a bite. With a parrot, take your time and progress through taming stages leisurely and gently. As you do, you will notice and learn to recognize its expressions of trust, fear, anger and so forth. Your bird will show its feelings through its face, eyes and carriage—just as you do! In a very short time your pet's personality will unfold and no longer be a mystery.

Oddly enough, biting is more likely to become a concern *after* a bird is tamed. This is true because the bird will have lost its fear of you and vice versa. As a result, you might become more aggressive and perhaps less courteous in your general handling of your pet. The bird might then repay you with a nip. (Again, biting might never occur with *your* pet.) According to Rosemary Low, Amazon parrots are prone to display this kind of behavior, call it unsteadiness, unpredictability or unreliability. These birds require consistent patience and gentle handling at all times. She, therefore, does not recommend Amazons as children's pets.

I once owned a very tame and gentle Severe Macaw. This bird apparently hated to be caged and hated more any intrusion in the cage. When I changed the feed cups, from the outside, the bird would viciously attack my fingers! Outside the cage, this particular bird was so gentle, I trusted it to preen my eyelashes—in spite of its enormous beak. I also owned tame cockatiels that would nip my fingers if I stopped petting them before they were satisfied! The point is that if biting arises with your tame pet, more often than not it will be a reaction to specific circumstances peculiar to your pet. You will be able to predict, handle and/or avoid it. With enough "bird know-how" you may even be successful at curing it. In any event, don't worry about it at this point.

ROOSTING

During the course of a day, birds seek out a safe, high perch and simply nap. A caged bird is no different. If your pet is sitting quietly or napping, don't disturb it. If you must, alert the bird first so you won't startle it. Actually say the bird's name and tell it what you plan to do. This may sound silly, but the less you surprise the bird, the more it will come to trust you.

A sleeping bird usually sits on one leg with its head tucked on its back. A bird in this position is slumped on its standing leg and the feathers of the chest are puffed, making the bird look fatter than usual. Some parrot-like birds like to snooze in a high corner, literally attached by feet and beak to the cage wires. On the other hand, a bird that is sitting puffed up on the perch during the day could be sick. A sick bird usually *looks* sick. It will be puffed up, its eyes will perhaps be half closed, it may have difficulty breathing, and it will stand on *both* feet. If your bird ever sits like this, it is important to *act quickly*. See Chapter 4 for help.

In general, it's a good idea to watch your bird for a few days (after it is settled, of course) just to discover its routine. Birds, like other animals, are *creatures of habit* and tend to repeat the same actions daily. Discover when your bird likes to roost, and then don't bother it. There are certain times, like roosting time, when even the tamest pet will resent your interferences. Accept this and honor your pet's privacy.

If your bird were in its natural habitat, it would awake with the sunrise and go to sleep with the sunset. In captivity, it is very important to ensure that your bird gets enough rest because a bird that is routinely subjected to days of various lengths will often develop metabolic disorders. Hormone functions, such as molting and breeding, are initiated by gradual changes in the length of the day. As long as there is light, it's daytime as far as a bird is concerned. This includes light from a television set, lamp, or fireplace! So, your bird should always receive light proportionate to the length of day as is occurring naturally outdoors. Whenever a light is on in the bird's room when it is dark outside, the bird should be covered enough to be in the dark.

Alternatively, if you cannot consistently cover and uncover your bird to correspond with the presence of the sun, you can simply ensure that your bird gets the opportunity for eight hours of uninterrupted sleep during the summer and twelve hours during the winter. During the spring and fall, you would increase and decrease, respectively, the length of the bird's day very gradually throughout the season. Simply cover the bird cage on a schedule that is convenient for you to follow every day.

When you put your pet to bed at night, it is a courtesy to make sure that the bird has eaten and gotten to its preferred roosting location before you completely darken its room. In nature, your bird would take the setting sun as its cue to fill up before total darkness. And, in the half-light, your bird might decide to move to a higher perch and slip in the sudden darkness. The result would be incredible panic—wild thrashing about the cage. After one of these episodes, you will not want a repeat performance!

For reasons which should be obvious by now, never allow anyone to disturb your bird in the dark while it's sleeping. Evening visitors are the usual culprits. Either keep the cage area lit or tell visitors frankly not to disturb your pet. After all, your pet is not a toy to be played with as the mood strikes, nor are you running a zoo!

A Hyacinthine Macaw from the San Diego Zoo takes a nap. Note the position, standing on one foot with the head on its back. Credit: Jean M. Hawthorne.

PERSONALITIES

Although your research of species characteristics will provide a description of what is normal behavior for your pet, *every bird is an individual.* Some budgies, for example, are fearless and outgoing, while others are quite timid. Some parrots will eat anything you offer; others will refuse a normal component of their diet—for instance, the corn in the parrot mix. Some conures and macaws will scream endlessly; others will be fairly quiet. The differences in behavior among birds of the same species could fill a very long list!

Observe your bird and adjust your handling of it to suit its personality. If your pet is timid, be extra patient and slow to make changes that might upset the bird. If your bird shows fear of toys, don't clutter the cage with them. The bird will not get over its fear by being afraid. Introduce toys one at a time gradually, preferably in a setting where the bird can get away from the offending object if it wants.

Once your pet is tamed, be prepared for more displays of individualism. Your previously timid bird might fly to anyone. Your outgoing bird might decide to show attention only to you. Some birds will single out one person for any reason and be nasty to him. It could be Aunt Helen because she has red hair; your wife because she pays "too much" attention to you; your neighbor who wears glasses; or you whenever you wear a certain garment. As in human relations, it is usually a waste of time to try to change personality. Acceptance is best.

BIRD INTELLIGENCE

No doubt, certain kinds of birds, like parrots, seem to be more intelligent than others. (Macaws and cockatoos are widely believed to be highly intelligent.) Obviously, a large parrot has more cranial capacity than a tiny finch. However, a parrot also has unique bodily characteristics, for example, the shape of its tongue, its toe arrangement, beak development, and pure size, that allow for differences in behavior. A parrot can learn to talk and perform amusing tricks with its feet and beak. A canary cannot. Who's to say which bird is more intelligent? Let's just say the parrot is more versatile.

No bird has reasoning power. A bird is a bundle of instincts and acquired habits. Birds, which have short attention spans, "learn" through repetition. So, if you want to tame your bird, you must show it over and over again that you can be trusted. If you want to train your bird, you must provide the same stimulus over and over again until it learns the habit. If your neighbor's parrot seems more clever than yours, it probably means your neighbor provided more stimuli on a regular, routine basis than you did. Your bird's only limitations will be its own body characteristics and the scope of stimuli provided repetitiously by you. It's that simple. Using your knowledge of bird behavior to help you and routinely providing stimuli under controlled conditions, you will train your bird to do as much as possible.

One final note: Because a bird cannot reason, do NOT, under any circumstances, attempt to punish the bird. Your bird will react to punishment with confusion and hostility, and you will only ruin the rapport you have developed. Punishment will get you nowhere fast. This is a guarantee! If you want to change your bird's behavior, use *your* reasoning power to examine the causes of the behavior and consistently remove them. Bad habits are hard to break, but they can be broken in time. Don't give up! By careful planning of your bird's routine, you can avoid most problems *before* they have a chance to develop into habits.

MOLTING

Molting is a natural process of shedding old feathers for new. It is not an illness. A bird that is molting loses only a few feathers at a time. There are never any bald spots on a molting bird nor are its flight capabilities ever impaired. Small birds first molt at about six months of age. Larger birds may not begin to molt until they are a year old. After a bird's first molt, it will molt again, year after year, during late summer or early fall and perhaps again before spring. (Dimorphic birds usually molt twice a year. These are the birds that assume some sort of "nuptial plumage" for the breeding season: bright colors, long tails, and so forth.) Parrots, however, seem to molt over a longer period, shedding their feathers only gradually.

Molting involves a certain amount of physical stress for birds, because the production of new feathers demands extra energy. During this period your male canary as well as other singing finches will not sing. There is no remedy for this. To tide your pet bird over its molt, provide extra varieties of seed and foods and make sure your bird gets adequate vitamins, exercise and rest.

A normal molt can last up to three months. If your bird molts continuously, check its surroundings for the cause. Your bird may not be getting adequate ventilation during hot spells or perhaps its cage is too close to a heater. A common mistake causing continuous molting is placing a bird's cage directly in front of a window. Occasional direct sunlight is great for your bird. It makes the manufacture of vitamin D possible. But sunshine through glass intensifies the heat of the sun's rays and triggers unnatural molting. If the situation is left uncorrected, your bird's strength will be dangerously sapped. If your bird decides to bask in the sunshine on your windowsill, however, trust the bird to know when it has had enough.

BREEDING INSTINCTS

The development of breeding instincts in young birds completes their lifelong, instinctual bag of tricks. Once a male bird develops the urge to breed, it will exhibit aggressive courting displays. Some birds come into dazzling color (like weavers), others develop extra feathers (like the long tails of whydahs) and others display what they have with newfound vigor (like outstretched wings, ruffled head and neck feathers, little dances, elaborate nest building, new songs and calls, and feeding regurgitated food). Most birds become hyperactive when they come into breeding condition. Canaries, in particular, are constantly hopping around during this period. Hens (broadly, female birds) generally show their breeding desires by nest building, mutual feeding, cooing and even laying sterile eggs.

Household pets show similar inclinations to mate and breed. It is common, for instance, to see a budgie flirting with its own reflection and regurgitating food on a favorite toy or mirror. An occasional bird will even regurgitate on its beloved owner. (Don't be upset if your bird expresses this fondness for you. It's only wet, hulled seeds.) Although it's sometimes sad to see your pet trying so hard and getting nowhere, don't be alarmed by its unusual behavior. Regurgitation under these conditions is perfectly normal; it does not forewarn of disease. When spring turns to fall and the daylight gradually lessens, so too will your pet's breeding urges.

Of course, we have no way of knowing if a pet's stifled breeding urges cause it mental or physical stress. Perhaps they do. I once had a Napoleon Weaver who was so eager to breed, he nested with a canary hen in totally unsuitable conditions. (Nothing came of this mating, by the way.) I know that my birds' inability to breed causes *me* stress!

I have had plenty of birds that survived not breeding, with no apparent damage. Many hens lay eggs, too. Merely laying an egg puts little stress on the hen. It is caring for chicks that is taxing. If your hen lays eggs, don't worry. She does not have to go on to incubation. Just remove the eggs as they are laid.

Sometimes a pet bird chooses its owner as its mate and directs all manner of affections to him. The behaviors can include displays, cooing or screeching, preening, regurgitation and even attempted copulation. These birds might also become protective, biting someone who comes too close to the human "mate" or even biting the mate in an attempt to drive him to safety (the imaginary "nest"). A bird does not have to have been handfed in order to reach this plateau of human-bird relations. Any bird can act this way. Just being aware of this possibility will help you handle the situation should it arise.

Different species of birds first come into breeding condition at different times, roughly related to their life spans. Then the urges continue in a cycle year after year, usually appearing in the spring. (Many Australian birds come into breeding condition in the fall, in spite of the fact that they have been bred in this hemisphere for many generations.) For example, a Zebra Finch may first show the desire to breed at only three to four months of age, although its body would not be sufficiently developed to care for healthy chicks until six to eight months of age. A budgie may develop the urge at around six to eight months (but is usually made to wait until at least twelve months by its well-intentioned keeper). Large parrots develop these urges much later, from two to five years old or more.

In general, a bird that has not developed the breeding urge, which is observable, is the best candidate for taming. Perhaps it is more receptive because its "birdie instincts" are incomplete. At any rate, this fact will give you an idea of the length of your bird's prime-time for taming. With a two-month-old budgie, you would have a full four months in which to work. With a parrot, your bird should be completely receptive to taming for two to five years. So, don't be overanxious for quick results. Although four months may seem like a long time to tame a budgie (and taming will probably not take that long), in terms of a life span of seven to twelve years, it's really very short. Of course, you can still tame a bird that has fully matured, but it generally requires more work and more patience.

By now you should have a good idea of your bird's behavior and preferences. Use this knowledge to help your taming and training efforts. Avoid going against what is natural to your pet and you will avoid unnecessary problems.

CHAPTER 3

Feeding

This chapter addresses two basic issues of bird care: what to feed and how to feed. *What to feed* is covered under two broad divisions: food for seed-eating birds and food for softbilled birds. These subjects are further divided between what I call the "staple diet" (the minimum fare) and the extras. *How to feed* to ensure your pet's health and to obtain maximum taming benefits is then discussed.

BASIC DIETS OF SEED-EATING BIRDS

The staple diets of seed-eating birds—hardbills and hookbills—are simple and well known. A basic seed mixture exists for each of the various types of birds discussed in this book and these mixtures are listed in the feeding tables included in this chapter. The staple diets are our approximations of the nutritional needs of various birds. They are essentially domesticated diets. It is highly doubtful, for instance, that any wild parrots eat sunflower seeds, although sunflower is the largest component of the household parrot's diet. Nevertheless, these diets have been fed to caged birds for many years and have demonstrated their abilities to keep birds healthy.

In addition to the basic seed mixtures, these birds require a constant supply of fresh, clean water, suitably sized gravel, cuttlebone and a vitamin supplement. Some birds can survive on just these elements of diet, but it is questionable for how long or in what state of health or bliss. So, it is beneficial, and also part of the fun of owning a bird, to feed at least a few of the supplementary foods. These will be explained in the following section.

It is important that the seeds you offer your pet be clean, fresh and *alive*. Stale seeds provide no food value. To ensure that your seeds are fresh, buy in small quantities and store them in a ventilated container so the seeds can "breathe." A coffee can with holes poked in the lid is good.

When you first establish a source for birdseed, it is a good idea to check the seeds' quality by planting some in a flowerpot. Stale seeds do not germinate. Fresh seeds do. You do not have to count out seeds, then plants, and determine the exact percentage of germination. But you should have a good idea of roughly how many seeds were planted compared to what grows. If little or no plants appear, throw away the seeds and buy new ones, perhaps from another source. (Planted birdseed is a good supplementary food. Feed your pet the results of your experiment—right from the pot.) Replant to test the quality of seeds from time to time or whenever your pet empties its dish by throwing uneaten seeds around the cage. Perhaps it is trying to tell you something.

Good sources of birdseed include bird stores, feed stores, petshops and, sometimes, grocery stores. Health food stores provide unsalted pumpkin seeds, *raw* peanuts and very clean sunflower seeds (which are worth a special trip if your grocer sells sunflower fit only for wild birds—very dirty seed). If you can't find a good source of seed in your area, you can order seed by mail from stores advertised in bird-oriented periodicals. See "Suggested Reading" at the end of this book.

In addition to the birds' staple diets, seed-eaters require a constant supply of fresh, clean water. Wash your pet's water container as often and as scrupulously as your own drinking glasses. Since birds often develop the nasty habit of dunking food into their water, it will sometimes foul before you would ordinarily replace it—especially in hot weather. Therefore, check and replace it whenever necessary. As a rule, check the water supply at least once a day. Without water, a small bird will die in about twenty-four hours.

For digestion, all seed-eating birds require gravel (also called health grit). Birds do not chew their food; they swallow whole or broken bits of seed and eat gravel. The gravel and the action of the gizzard (equivalent to your stomach) then grind the consumed seed. Gravel comes in different sizes or grades for small and large birds. A good health grit is composed of crushed granite and small amounts of oyster shell and charcoal. It provides trace minerals.

Gravel should not be sprinkled over the floor of the cage because it will be soiled by the bird's droppings. It should be served in a small cup and checked occasionally to make sure it has not become impacted and unpalatable.

Because the function of gravel is to grind food, not to provide scratching pleasure, *never substitute kitty litter*. Kitty litter is supposed to absorb moisture, so it is composed of clay. In your bird's crop and gizzard, kitty litter would pulverize to mud!

Another form of "gravel" which is not suitable is the sort that is glued to cage paper and perch covers. This gravel is too fine to be of any grinding use and because it is on the floor of the cage it is likely to be soiled by the bird's droppings. Ingesting the glue by which the gravel is stuck to the paper is of dubious value, too. There is really no point in

A good bird store offers a variety of birdseed for your special pet. This display was photographed at Birds in Paradise, Flushing, NY. Credit: Peter Sutherland.

providing gravel this way, so it is a waste of money to purchase these products. In addition, gravel paper and, especially, perch covers are quite irritating to the feet. A perch cover is like sandpaper insoles for your shoes. You wouldn't use them; neither should your pet.

Cuttlebone, which is the backbone of the cuttlefish, should be supplied to all seed-eating birds. It not only provides calcium and salts, but also helps to keep the beak trim. A substitute for cuttlebone is a mineral block. Mineral blocks are simply plaster: lime (calcium oxide) and sand. If you wanted to take the trouble, you could make your own mineral blocks from plaster of Paris. Another homemade source of usable calcium is crushed eggshells. You can save the shells from your hardcooked eggs and crush them with a rolling pin. Then add them to your pet's gravel.

Vitamins *made especially for birds* should also be given to your pet every day. These vitamins come in liquids to add to the bird's drinking water or powders to mix with the birdseed. I find the powders easier to administer and less expensive.

Table 1: Finches

Staple Diet
Finch mix (small red and white millet, canary seed and oats)

Extras
Spray millet
Canary songfood mix
Any commercial variety seed mix (conditioning food, molting food, treat food, etc., sold for canaries and budgies)
Safflower seeds (large finches only)
Wild-gathered seeding grasses
Sprouted or rooted birdseed
Leafy greens (carrot tops, spinach, dandelion, etc.)
Uncooked, fresh vegetables (corn on the cob, peas, cucumber, etc.)
Fruits (apples, oranges, peaches, berries, bananas, etc.)
A clean clump of sod (grass, roots and earth)
Alfalfa cubes (sold for hamsters and other small animals)
Hardcooked egg
Peanut butter
Mealworms (sparingly, only two or three per day)
Nectar food

Table 2: Pigeons and Doves*

Staple Diet

Pigeon mix (corn, Canadian or cow peas, red wheat, buckwheat, kafir corn, barley, hemp seed)

OR

Pigeon pellets (a manufactured, grain-based diet with vitamins)

Alternative Staple Diet for Small Doves

Budgie or finch mix (millet, canary seed and oats)

Extras

Budgie mix
Safflower seeds
Wild-gathered seeding grasses
Sprouted or rooted birdseed
A clean clump of sod (grass, roots and earth)
Alfalfa cubes (sold for hamsters and other small animals)
Leafy greens (carrot tops, spinach, dandelion, etc.)
Uncooked, fresh vegetables (peas, cucumber, etc.)
Chicken scratch (cracked corn)

* Certain foreign pigeons and doves require a softbill diet. See the following sections.

Table 3: Canaries

Staple Diet

Canary mix (canary and rape seeds)

Extras

Same as finch extras (see Table 1), except no mealworms
Color food (red-ground birds only)

Table 4: Budgies

Staple Diet

Budgie/Parakeet mix (millet, canary seed and oats)

Extras

Same as finch extras (see Table 1), except no mealworms
Cracked sunflower seeds

Table 5: Lovebirds

Staple Diet

By volume:
   1 part budgie/parakeet mix (millet, canary seed and oats)
   2 parts sunflower seeds

Extras

Same as finch extras (see Table 1), except no mealworms

Table 6: Cockatiels

Staple Diet

By volume:
   1 part budgie/parakeet mix (millet, canary seed and oats)
   1 part sunflower seeds

Extras

Same as finch extras (see Table 1), except no mealworms

Table 7: Conures and Parrots

Staple Diet

Parrot mix (sunflower, millet, oats, raw peanuts in the shell, dried red-hot
   peppers, corn, pumpkin seeds, safflower seeds)

Extras

Same as finch extras (see Table 1)
Pigeon mix
Chicken scratch (cracked corn)
Turkey pellets
Budgie mix (if not included in parrot mix)
Raw peanuts in the shell (in addition to the parrot mixture)
Shelled walnuts
Other nuts (unsalted, in the shell)
Dog biscuits, dog kibble
Mealworms (not accepted by most parrots)
Dry bread (may be toasted; jelly, jam or peanut butter may be applied)

Amazon Parrots (*left*, Spectacled Amazon; *right*, Finsch's Amazon). Photo by Peter Sutherland.

Blue-Fronted Amazon. Photo by Peter Sutherland.

Triton Cockatoos. Photo by Jean M. Hawthorne.

African Gray Parrots. Photo by Peter Sutherland.

Left, Blue and Gold Macaw; *center*, White-Eyed Conure; *right*, Severe Macaw. Photo by Peter Sutherland.

Mitred Conure. Photo by Jean M. Hawthorne.

Greater Indian Hill Mynah. Photo by Jean M. Hawthorne.

SUPPLEMENTARY FOODS FOR SEED-EATING BIRDS

Feeding your bird should be a simple matter. Do not let the length of the list of extra foods intimidate you from owning a bird. The length of the list merely points out the great variety of extras that you may offer your pet, though only rarely will a single bird accept all these different foods. Keep in mind that these foods are extras; they should not be fed in such abundance that the bird neglects its basic fare.

Seed Extras.   Spray millet, which is millet seed on the stem of the plant, is relished by finches, canaries and hookbills. Even some macaws like spray millet, although eating the tiny seeds may seem impossible for these big-beaked birds.

Canary songfood mix should be supplied year-round to all canaries (both sexes); it is also liked by most finches and small hookbills. It is a stimulating seed and will prompt singing birds to begin singing sooner and longer if the supply is increased during the latter part of the molt.

"Variety seeds" are packaged seeds for canaries and budgies under various labels—for example, treat food, conditioning food or molting food. They can be fed to *any* seed-eating bird. These are beneficial seed mixtures. However, before purchasing two or three kinds for your pet, check the ingredients statements. Many of these mixtures contain essentially the same seeds in the same proportions. As you may know, the first item on the ingredients statement represents the largest component of the mix; the second item, the next largest by volume; and so on. Reading the labels can save you some money and your bird some monotony!

Oat groats are usually packaged and sold along with other variety seeds. Oat groats are just hulled oat seeds. If they are already present in your pet's seed mixture, there is no need to purchase extras. Oats are regarded as fattening seeds and should not be fed in great quantities often.

Safflower seeds are excellent and can even be substituted for sunflower as the largest seed component of the diet for hookbills. Safflower does wonders for plumage. The shell of this seed is very tough, so little birds might not be able to crack it. Ask your petshop for a small sample to see if your bird can eat it before you buy in quantity.

Seeding grasses can be gathered during an excursion in undeveloped fields or even from patches of weeds in your neighborhood. Avoid areas where plants may have been sprayed with insecticides or otherwise contaminated.

Greens.   Sprouted birdseed is a highly beneficial food, and most birds love it. To sprout seeds, place about a tablespoon of seeds in a glass jar, add enough water to cover the seeds, and cover the top with cheesecloth secured by a rubber band. Allow the seeds to soak overnight. Then pour off the water (through the cheesecloth) and rinse the seeds in clean water. Drain off the water again, shake the jar to distribute the seeds and place the jar on its side in a warm, dark spot. (A towel thrown over the jar will produce these conditions.) Rinse and drain the seeds three or four times a day until they are ready to harvest, usually in two or three days.

Sprouting seeds is a good way to cajole your pet into eating seeds basic to its diet that it doesn't seem to care for. For example, if your canary refuses to eat rape seed, sprout some and see if it makes a difference. It probably will.

Planted birdseed is a good form of green food, too. It is the only way (other than sprouting, of course) to test if your seeds are fresh, until you develop a "nose" for the aroma of fresh seed. It is a safe substitute for a clump of sod, providing "grass," roots and earth that you know is unharmed by weed killers, pesticides, dog and cat refuse and other harmful chemicals.

Dehydrated greens for birds are also available. Like fresh greens, dehydrated greens are rich in calcium and minerals. They are simply mixed with the birdseed. These greens are the easiest to feed to your bird, but they are also the least fun to eat. Many birds will ignore them. On the other hand, alfalfa cubes will tempt many birds. These cubes are usually sold for hamsters and other small animals in petshops. They look like little green bales of hay and are very aromatic. Parrots that won't touch other greens sometimes like them.

Greens in one form or another should be fed to your pet regularly. In general, the darker the green, the more nutritious the vegetable for your pet. Carrot tops, spinach, dandelion, chickory, cress and chickweed are good examples. Even cut grass is a good green food for your pet. Iceberg lettuce and other light-colored vegetables provide comparatively less nutrition, but these are better than nothing. If you have only lettuce on hand, by all means serve it. Your bird will love it.

As a rule, *always thoroughly rinse* any greens, vegetables and fruit fed to your bird to remove harmful chemicals. Even if you pick them from your own garden, you can't be sure of what's blown over from your neighbor's yard or what four-legged creature has left its calling card. To be safe, rinse thoroughly.

Contrary to popular belief, green foods that are eaten regularly do not cause diarrhea. They do help deter your bird from nibbling on your houseplants! Greens and fruits will make your bird's droppings more runny than otherwise, but this is extra water, not disease.

Other Vegetables.   Most vegetables are suitable as bird food. Little birds can handle wedges of cucumber (served seed side up), corn on the cob,

Freep, a gray cockatiel hen, shares some grapefruit for breakfast. Credit: Don Hunsaker II.

and grated carrot. Pigeons, doves and hookbills can eat fresh peas. Larger hookbills, like conures and parrots, can hold food in their feet, so larger vegetables (green beans, carrot sticks, celery sticks, small onions, hot peppers, etc.) can be served to them. Cucumbers, onions, and so forth should be peeled. Again, rinse thoroughly.

Fruits. Fruits should be washed as a matter of routine. Tough-skinned fruits, like apples and pears, should be served peeled. Fruits that would fall apart if peeled, like berries, grapes or plums, can be halved or quartered. Citrus fruits need not be peeled either. They should be sliced to expose a small part of each section for tiny birds and served in wedges to larger birds. Try to offer some variety. An orange every day is not good and becomes monotonous.

Dog Biscuits or Dry Dog Food Kibble. Most parrots love to play with dog biscuits; they even eat part of them! These biscuits are usually the bird's only source of animal protein, so they are a valuable dietary addition. A biscuit every other day is a good schedule. The best kind to serve, either plain or colored, are sold in bulk by the pound in petshops. Parrots are usually more interested in the colored bones.

Some parrot mixes contain dry dog food nuggets. If the bird eats them, there is no dietary need to supply further animal protein in the form of dog biscuits. However, many parrots do not touch the dry nuggets but relish the biscuits. Perhaps it is a matter of shape.

Nuts. Most conures and parrots become rather addicted to peanuts. They are highly nutritious but should be rationed so the bird eats enough of its other foods. Raw peanuts are preferable to roasted, which are oilier. To preserve the value of peanuts as extras, remove them from your parrot's staple mixture and feed them directly as treats.

Large hookbills will accept other nuts in the shell, like walnuts, pecans or filberts. If the bird doesn't get the idea to eat the nut, crack it first and present the shattered shell with nutmeat. Do not feed salted nuts.

Peanut butter is also beneficial. If your pet will not eat it plain, try spreading it on a piece of cracker or toast.

Eggs. The best food for fish is fish; likewise, egg is a good food for birds. The egg should be hardcooked (about ten minutes) and served grated or mashed. Bread crumbs can be added to produce a crumble texture.

Eggs should be fed in portions that will be eaten immediately because eggs can spoil quickly, especially in hot weather. When spoiled, eggs are lethal. So, take care that your pet does not scatter the egg around the cage for snacking later.

Insects. Many finches require some sort of live food (animal protein). Any bird that will eat insects will benefit from them; for example, European fanciers feed mealworms to their canaries. The easiest "insect" to feed is the mealworm. Mealworms are available from most petshops or by mail and are quite inexpensive. Caged birds that require live food will gorge themselves on mealworms if allowed, so you should ration them. I doubt that there is any danger of a bird becoming "fat" by eating too many mealworms (they are almost pure protein and water); the danger is that the diet will be thrown out of proportion. A caged bird needs only so much energy and mealworms are capable of providing more than enough of it.

Take care that your bird actually eats the worm instead of dropping it on the cage floor, where it might escape. (These worms are not very fast, but they sometimes manage to break loose.) This sometimes happens when the bird has plenty more in its dish, so—why bother to go after it?

Mealworms are the larval stage in the life cycle of a brown beetle. After the worm comes the pupa stage, a dormant cocoon existence from which the beetle hatches. The birds usually don't touch the pupa or the beetle, and you will not want to either!

You may be wondering at this point whether your finch's need for animal protein can be met by a less repulsive source than live insects. Obviously, parrots can fulfill this need by eating nifty little biscuits. The answer is yes. There are a few inanimate substitutes for live food. The problem with inanimate food is that some birds will not touch it; they want a food that moves or none at all. If you'd like to try anyway, see the description of insectile meal and others in the softbill feeding section that follows.

A few other insects that your bird might like are available commercially. See the supplementary foods description for softbilled birds.

Nectar. Feeding nectar to most hookbills (Lories and Lorikeets require it) and to hardbills is simply something nice you do for the bird. It is not necessary. Nectar provides easily assimilated food value and is basically a gourmet treat. Nectar recipes vary from the simple solutions of either plain white sugar or honey with water to more elaborate concoctions of honey, water, soya powder, evaporated milk, beef bouillon, baby food and other ingredients.

As a special treat, once in a while, mix a small amount of honey with water (say, 25 percent honey to 75 percent water) and serve it in a container separate from the bird's water. Let the bird refuse the nectar without having to refuse its water.

Color Food. Red-ground birds, particularly Red-Factor Canaries, are often fed color-enhancing agents like carotenoids and canthaxanthin to maintain their depth of color from molt to molt. There are many brands of color "foods" on the market and they are usually added to the bird's drinking water. Mixing and feeding directions are supplied by the manufacturers.

It is a widespread, though not universal, practice to administer these coloring agents daily, just before and during the annual molt. Daily feeding ensures the evenness of color through the feathers. Your bird's health will *not* be affected if you do not serve color food; it is strictly an option. However, if you buy a Red-Factor Canary because you are impressed by the bird's intense color, you may be disappointed after it molts if you do not provide this extra.

Other Extras.   Some resourceful parrot owners are using sweet feed intended for horses (e.g., Purina Omalene) as a treat for parrots. The feed contains soybean meal, which boosts the parrot's protein intake, and is quite palatable because of its molasses content. It also contains cracked corn and oats, both good for birds. If you can obtain a small quantity of such feed, try it! Most seeds are very marginal in protein content and parrots usually won't eat soybeans or mealworms to improve their diets.

Many other suggestions for extra foods can be found in other bird books and you may think of more yourself. If you have any doubt about the advisability of feeding *any* food, check with your veterinarian by all means. Since there are so many good extra foods to feed your pet, try to resist the temptation to offer your bird potato chips, pretzels, Cracker Jack, scrambled eggs, mashed potatoes and the like; it may lead to trouble.

BASIC DIETS OF SOFTBILLED BIRDS

Softbilled birds are usually classed in one of five groups, depending on their major food requirements. The groups are: nectivores, frugivores, insectivores, carnivores and omnivores. Respectively, the birds in these groupings require predominantly: nectar, fruit, insects, meat and some of each of the preceding. A nectivorous bird requires more than just nectar, however. For example, the hummingbird, a nectivore, requires about fifteen fruit flies per day to meet its needs for animal protein. The Shama Thrush, an insectivore, also benefits from fruit and nectar. And so on. The research you do on your pet softbill will outline its dietary requirements. Realizing that your pet is a carnivore, omnivore or whatever, will enable you to choose the correct extras to supplement its diet.

Except for the nectivorous group, the major dietary requirements of most softbills are satisfied by a commercial mynah food mixture. Mynah food usually contains dehydrated fruits, animal and vegetable meals (i.e., grain meals and meat and bone meals), vitamins and minerals and easily digestible oils. The protein content of the typical brand is no less than 25 percent.

One possibly serious shortcoming of mynah food should be noted. Recent evidence suggests that pet mynahs that are fed *only* mynah food may develop internal disorders, including kidney and liver diseases. It is not the contents of the mixtures but *the lack of moisture in them* that may cause the trouble. In nature, mynahs consume a diet consisting of nearly 80 percent water, whereas commercially prepared mynah food contains only 10 to 20 percent moisture (if fresh). It is believed that the lack of moisture in the high protein mixtures puts unnatural strain on the bird's short digestive tract. That is, the bird is unable to absorb and metabolize the nutrients efficiently because of the lack of water in the artificial diet compared to the high water content of the natural diet. A partial solution to this problem is to provide varied, moisture-rich extras *regularly*.

Mynah food is available in meal, pellets and kibble (a crumble texture). Pellets are the easiest to administer and are accepted by softbills as small as Pekin Robins. Meals require moistening with water or grated apple or carrot.

Along with the mynah food, water should be constantly available. Nothing else is necessary except for the daily offering of one or two moisture-rich extras to keep the bird in tiptop shape and to bring about and maintain tameness. The portion size of the extra depends on the species. Additional homework is advised. Softbills should not be fed seeds of any kind and do not need cuttlebone or grit. If the mynah food contains vitamins and minerals, as it usually does, no vitamin supplement is necessary. If you are in doubt about the quality or vitamin content of your mynah mix, ask your veterinarian to review the ingredients statement. He will be able to tell you if the mix is deficient in any way.

If you have decided to keep hummingbirds, the diet is simply nectar and fruit flies. The birds get more than enough water in the nectar, so no extra water need be furnished. A recipe for hummingbird nectar is supplied in the following section.

SUPPLEMENTARY FOODS FOR SOFTBILLED BIRDS

The items of diet listed as "Extras" in the feeding chart for softbills (Table 8) could be substituted for mynah food as a complete diet, if the various items were fed in the correct proportions for the various softbills. Of course, it is much simpler to feed mynah pellets and supplement the diet according to the bird's needs and wants. For example, an insectivore will need extra animal protein in the form of insects. A carnivore or an omnivore should receive even greater concentrations of animal protein in the form of raw meat. All the birds, except hummingbirds, need fresh fruit.

Table 8: Softbilled Birds*

Basic Diet
Mynah food (meal, pellets or kibble)

Extras
Fruit (apples, oranges, tomatoes, melons, bananas, avocadoes, berries, soaked raisins, peaches, plums, etc.)
Cooked and cooled carrots or sweet potatoes or yams
Insectile meal
Dry dog food
New World monkey chow
Raw meat (e.g., lean chopped beef, horsemeat)
Live food (e.g., newborn mice, day-old chicks)
"Insects" (e.g., mealworms, white worms, fruit flies, crickets, aphides, spiders, etc.)
Cheese
Hardcooked egg
Peanut butter
Nectar

* Different species of softbilled birds will have varying diet requirements. Be sure to check your pet's species' requirements during your research. *Do not rely solely on this list.*

Fruit. Fruit should be fed peeled and diced into bite-size pieces, like the size of the fruit in the typical, commercially canned fruit cocktail. Citrus fruits and fruits that would fall apart if peeled, like tomatoes and plums, can be fed with the skins. These fruits should be cut in half so the bird can peck at the exposed centers. Large grapes and berries should be cut in half or quartered.

When fresh fruits are out of season or temporarily unavailable, raisins or other dried fruits that have been softened by soaking in water overnight can be fed to your bird. As a last resort, canned fruit cocktail can be used if carefully rinsed to remove the heavy, sugary syrup. Uneaten fruits should be discarded before they spoil.

Try to feed a variety of fruits. Feeding one or two kinds all the time defeats the purpose.

Insectile Meal, Dry Dog Food and Monkey Chow. Many bird books suggest feeding insectile meal without explaining what it is. Insectile meal is simply a coarse textured meal made from animal and vegetable products. It usually contains grain meals (e.g., plain biscuit meal, whole-meal flour, soya flour) and "meat" meals (e.g., fish, shrimp, meat and

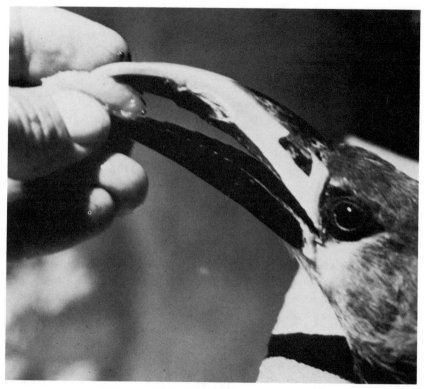

This toucanet gingerly accepts fruit from its owner's fingers. Credit: Don Hunsaker II.

bone meals) in the ratio of about 60 percent vegetable to 40 percent animal. Since insectile meal contains meat products, it is a source of animal protein.

If your local bird store does not stock insectile meal, you can make your own. Simply buy a dry dog or cat food with similar ingredients and grind the pellets into a coarse meal. Unfortunately, the ordinary household blenders or food processors are usually not heavy-duty enough to handle this grinding job. A coffee grinder may be necessary.

New World monkey chow may be fed as a supplemental food, too. It is manufactured by many feed producers (Purina, Wayne, Science Diet, etc.) and can be ordered by any petshop or feed store. Only New World monkey chow contains vitamin D in a form usable by birds. If you already feed an insectile meal in addition to mynah food, monkey chow would be redundant.

"Insects." Many types of "insects" are available commercially or can be gathered by hand. Certain kinds of insects, though, are not especially appealing to use if they can escape the bird and fly out of the cage. However, if a little ingenuity is applied to the feeding process, the birds usually learn to catch them. Try devising a container whereby only one insect is released at a time.

Mealworms are the easiest to feed to your bird. They are available cheaply from most petshops and bird stores or can be ordered by mail. These "worms" are the larval stage in the life cycle of a brown beetle and can be easily cultured at home. All that's needed is a container filled with red bran, available from a feed store, to which a little moisture is added in the form of a piece of apple, an apple core, or potato peels. The container should be deep enough to prevent the mealworms from crawling out. A few mealworms are dropped into this mixture, where they will complete their life cycle. In a month or so, depending on the temperature —higher temperatures speed up the life cycle—the young mealworms can be harvested. As long as there is food and moisture in the container, the mealworms will continue to reproduce indefinitely.

Fruit flies can be cultured at home, too. Rotting fruit (say melons or bananas) in the bottom of a coffee can will attract them and begin the culture. When flies start to appear, cover the container with wire mesh so that the insects can escape but the bird cannot reach the rotted fruit. The bird usually learns to sit by the container waiting for an insect to fly out, when it is quickly snapped up.

White worms are available from most tropical fish stores. Crickets are usually available from petshops that sell lizards. Some flying insects can be ordered from large plant nurseries or greenhouse operations.

Softbills will also eat ordinary earthworms, but they should not be fed to a bird since earthworms often carry parasites which can be transferred to the bird.

These birds will also devour cockroaches, maggots, spiders, house-flies and other disgusting creatures.

Cheese and Eggs.   Hard cheeses, like cheddar, can be fed grated as an occasional treat. Hardcooked eggs are also relished. Feed only small portions of egg, however, and take care to remove anything uneaten before it has a chance to spoil. Spoiled eggs are poisonous!

Peanut Butter.   Peanut butter is an excellent supplementary food. A small container of it can be left before the bird constantly, if desired.

Nectar.   Many recipes for nectar are found in many books. The usual ingredients are honey or plain white sugar; Gerval, a powdered protein containing vitamins and trace minerals, manufactured by Lederle; soya powder or evaporated milk; beef bouillon; other various additions; and, of course, water.

If your softbill requires nectar food, check with the seller regarding the ingredients of the nectar he has been feeding the bird. Then, rely on your research about your softbill to learn of other recipes—perhaps better, perhaps more convenient to prepare.

A simple recipe suitable for hummingbirds is one teaspoon of Gerval dissolved in a little warm water, four teaspoons of sugar dissolved in a little hot water, and enough additional water to make five ounces. This recipe can be changed to suit other nectivores by changing the amount of sugar or water added to the nectar. For example, a nectivore that eats insects and fruit will need less carbohydrates than are provided in the nectar recipe just described. To compensate, you could reduce the sugar content by half.

Fresh nectar should be supplied to nectivores in the early morning and removed at night. A solution of sugar and water should be available during the night. Feeding containers (use tube feeders, *not* open dishes) must be cleaned and disinfected after each use.

HOW TO FEED

Again, the staple items of diet should be available to the bird constantly. For seed-eaters, these items include the basic seed mixture, cuttlebone, grit, vitamins and water; for softbills, mynah pellets, vitamins and water. The feeders should be positioned so that food and water will not be soiled by the bird's droppings. A few arboreal birds may not be willing to eat food from containers placed on the cage floor. Watch out for little quirks.

The food supply should be checked daily. Most small seed-eaters crack their seeds and drop the husks back into the dish, creating the appearance of a full dish which, in fact, is empty. So, to prevent needless starvation, it is important to remove the husks and refill the container to its normal level. Husks can be removed by gently shaking the feed dish to settle the heavy ingredients (the good seed) to the bottom of the dish. Then, blow the top layer of husks directly into the garbage. Hookbills that consume a sunflower seed mixture will normally eat the entire contents of their food dish daily. Salvage what you can and refill. Mynah food that has been moistened for feeding should be thrown away if uneaten (at least daily but more often in hot weather) and the dish should be washed before refilling. Otherwise, the food will sour and become moldy, producing fatal results if eaten.

Most birds would rather starve than eat strange-looking food. Therefore, when you first purchase your pet, find out what it has been eating. If this food is not available in your area or different from what you want to use, obtain at least a two-week supply from the seller when you get the bird. Then feed this original mix and very gradually add the new feed to it until the bird is eventually eating only the new mixture. This gradual method should be used whenever you want to introduce a change in the bird's staple diet.

When feeding extras, remember: *Extras are extras!* Do not feed them in quantities that will make the bird reluctant to eat its staple diet.

Feeding extras will best work to your taming advantage if you always make it a habit to attract the bird's attention to these "goodies" rather than allowing the bird to discover them in the cage on its own. In this way, your bird will learn that "goodies" come *only* from you. During the period when you will be taming your pet, try to give extras especially during the bird's period of freedom. Then your pet will associate freedom and good things with you. This will be a major milestone in your taming effort.

Whenever possible, try to feed extras directly. Any bird that can eat a peanut, a mealworm or a grape can take it right from your fingers. Offer it! If the bird does not accept food this way, *then* place the treat in a special feeding cup. Use a special treat cup for little birds, too, like canaries, that cannot consume a morsel whole. This cup should look different from the cage feed cups. It should also be a different color. In a surprisingly short time, your pet will recognize that you are giving it something special, such as variety seeds or fruit, when it sees this cup.

Unfortunately, your bird will probably not accept everything you offer as extras. Birds can be slow to accept new or strangely colored foods. Keep trying and don't give up. Offer your pet a wedge of apple or orange, then place it in the treat cup. Perhaps the bird will associate the cup with other good things and try something new that is placed in it. Eventually, you will notice nibble marks on something or discover that bits of food are missing, and your bird will begin to show at least some preferences. Take note of what your bird seems to like best so that you can use it to tempt, coax or bribe your pet to trust you or to learn appropriate behavior or tricks.

CHAPTER 4

General Hygiene

This chapter provides hygiene guidelines for the care of both your bird and its cage. What to do in case of disease is discussed and a section is devoted to minor problems affecting your pet's health. Home remedies are suggested.

CAGE HYGIENE

To keep your bird's cage clean, you need only a few simple tools. I recommend a nipple or bottle brush to clean food and water containers. A brush is essential to clean nectar feeders. Another handy kitchen gadget is a basting brush (or a stiff artist's brush) to sweep the crevices of the cage, particularly where the cage wires meet the cage base. Keeping these areas clean will minimize dust and prolong the looks and life of the cage. Both of these items are available in a well-stocked supermarket. A butter knife will serve to scrape the perches.

It is a good practice to sponge down the cage once a week to remove particles of food or droppings from the cage wires. If left intact, this debris will corrode the plating on your cage very quickly. (Remove the bird first, of course, since you must sponge the insides, too.)

The floor lining where the bird's droppings will accumulate should be changed often, ideally once a day. The easiest way to ensure that this gets done is to precut a large quantity of the paper you want to use on the cage floor. Then, if you insert about seven sheets, you can simply remove the top sheet daily. When the last sheet is gone, it will remind you to sweep and sponge down the cage.

Suitable floor linings include plain paper, newspaper, precut cage paper (without gravel!) and bird litter. Although newspaper is cheap and widely available, it could spoil the appearance of a light-colored bird if the ink is not thoroughly dried. Also, there is a controversy that even scientific evidence has been unable to dispel about whether the ink is harmful to birds. To be on the safe and clean side, use only old newspapers, a week or more aged, in your pet's cage.

Bird litter is a relatively new product. It is composed of ground, sterile corncobs in pellet form. It is nontoxic to birds if eaten. Other well known litter material, like cedar shavings, pine shavings or sawdust, can produce harmful effects should the bird decide to eat them. They also have a tendency to blow away when the bird flaps its wings. Again, *never* use kitty litter! Litter material, in general, has a tendency to mask the bird's droppings, making it difficult to detect the onset of diarrhea and too easy to prolong the intervals between cleanings. Therefore, the use of paper as a floor lining is preferable and I recommend it.

Since your pet will be cleaning its beak on the perches, they must be kept clean also. Use a knife or wire brush to scrape off debris, or wash them in water the easy way. If you wash the perches, make sure they are completely dried before returning them to the cage, because damp perches can lead to foot trouble. Keeping two sets of perches to use in shifts, one in use, one being cleaned, is a good idea.

BIRD HYGIENE AND COMFORT

Naturally, you will want to keep your bird as clean as its cage, so offer baths frequently. In hot weather, a daily bath is ideal. My birds bathe many times a day during the summer, taking another dip as soon as they have dried off from the last bath. In cold weather, offer a bath only in a warm, draft-free room and restrict it to one to three times per week, depending on your bird's affinity toward bathing. Try to use water at room temperature, never hot or ice cold. And always offer baths during daylight so that your pet will be completely dry before it goes to sleep.

Keep your pet's toenails trimmed for safety's sake. It is common for a bird to catch its overgrown toenails on cage wires, carpeting, open-weave drapes and furniture, and even your clothing. If this happens, your bird will try to shake its foot loose and quickly panic. The result is often a broken toe or leg. If you already have a bird, check its toenails right away and trim them if needed. If you're planning to get a bird, have the breeder or petshop trim its nails if necessary.

For trimming you can use your own fingernail or toenail clippers, special bird-claw scissors or dog toenail clippers. The size of the bird will determine which clippers you should use. If you use your own nail clippers, cut across the thinnest portion of the nail so as not to shatter it.

To trim, gently grasp the bird bodily (wearing gloves, if necessary) and cut the nails one by one. It's a simple operation. Most birds have light-colored claws, so it's easy to see where the quick (blood-filled portion) stops. Always cut below the quick and your bird will feel no pain. Until you are confident of your toenail trimming skills, however, keep a capful of hydrogen peroxide near you in case you cut into the quick accidentally. If you or the bird is fidgety, this can happen. Dip the claw

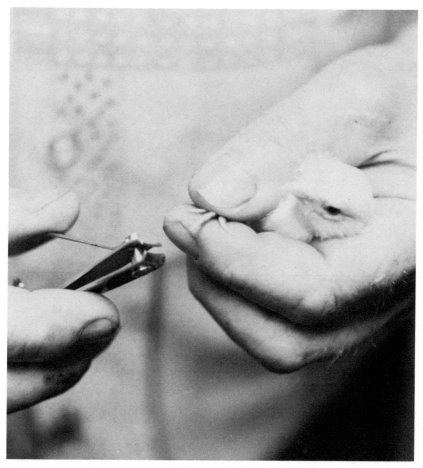

Veteran canary breeder Joe Marssdorf shows correct way to trim toenails, while the bird surveys the situation. Credit: Peter Sutherland.

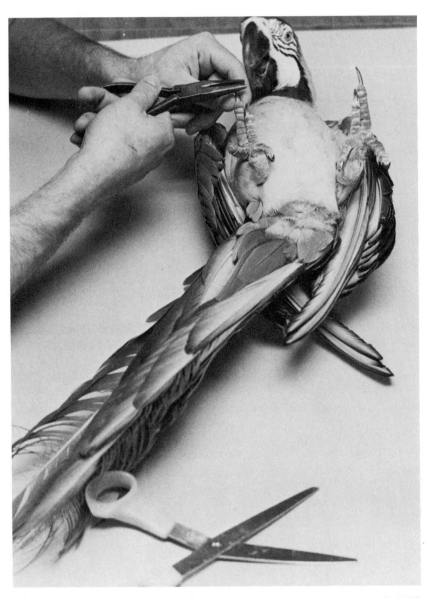

Unfortunately, birds are not usually as cooperative as this Blue and Gold Macaw, Pablo, for nail trimming! Credit: Peter Sutherland.

into the hydrogen peroxide to stop the bleeding, and be more careful. You can also use other coagulants on hand, like styptic powders or sticks of alum (powdered ammonium alum).

A tame small bird's toenails can be trimmed while it's sitting on your finger. Do it calmly and nonchalantly so you don't tip off your pet. Eight snips and it's over. If you have a large bird or a bird with black toenails, try to have someone with experience trim its nails. (Many bird stores offer this service.) Otherwise, have one person hold the bird while you trim. For black nails, cut just the tips. Naturally, with any bird, hold firmly but don't squeeze!

Unless your bird has its own room, you will need a cover for its bird cage to ensure that the bird gets enough sleep. A dark color is best because it allows the least amount of light to filter into the cage. If your parrot is adept at removing its cover, you might want to construct one that is tamper-proof. If so, make a wooden or wire frame larger than the cage and cover the frame with the cloth rather than the cage itself. Your pet will then not be able to reach the cloth. Round tablecloths, which come in a variety of colors and patterns to match any decor, are excellent parrot cage covers. Square cloths work also but, I think, do not drape as well.

Many people like to take their pet birds outdoors during mild weather. Indeed, the dream of every bird enthusiast (including me) is to be able to provide an aviary with outdoor flights so the birds can go outside at will. Pigeon fanciers often allow their birds to fly completely at liberty. However, there are other schools of thought on this subject. One is that pet birds simply do not need the change; it is only the birds' owners who think it is a kindness. Another more compelling reason exists. Dr. Leslie Zeman of Cornell University warns, "Pet birds can acquire several diseases from wild birds without direct contact, including parasites (lice and coccidia), blood parasites, viruses (domestic Newcastle disease and equine encephalitis) and bacteria. Mosquitoes, stray bird droppings and contaminated branches are sufficient to transmit disease."

These are the prevailing opinions, practices and facts. You must make your own decision. If you take your pet outside, be alert for signs of trouble and prepared for disappointments.

IF YOUR BIRD BECOMES ILL

As soon as you get your bird (better yet, *before*), find a veterinarian who specializes in avian medicine. Not all veterinarians possess equal skill with birds. To find one who does, ask your petshop dealer or bird breeder to recommend one. Or, ask a veterinarian you know directly. Then, figure out how you will transport the bird in an emergency. If transporting a very large bird will be a problem, try to find a veterinarian who is willing to come to *you*. Again, do this *before* an emergency!

Pet birds taken outdoors need protection from wind, cats, dogs, vandals and the hot sun. Credit: Jean M. Hawthorne.

In general, birds that are cared for properly rarely become ill. For their size, birds are very hardy. However, if your bird suddenly displays unusual symptoms (for instance, runny or blocked nostrils, frequent sneezing, diarrhea, sudden loss of weight, disinterest in food, difficulty in breathing, wheezing or sores) or is injured, try to make the bird warm as a first aid measure and call your veterinarian *immediately* for advice and treatment.

To warm the bird, place a cover over the cage, leaving one side exposed. Place the exposed side near a low-wattage light bulb (twenty-five or forty watts). (If you can obtain a green light bulb, do so as it will be less irritating to the eyes.) The bulb will throw off heat and gradually raise the temperature in the cage. Ninety degrees Fahrenheit will produce the best results. Temperatures over 95 degrees Fahrenheit could be dangerous; use a thermometer to determine the cage temperature.

Alternatively, you can place the covered cage on top of a heating pad to raise the cage temperature. If you do, remove perches at the top of the cage, so your bird will be forced to sit near the heat source.

When your bird is distressed, external heat is recommended to make up for lost body heat. Caloric energy produces body heat, and a sick bird has less energy to spare maintaining its normal body temperature.

Don't be in a hurry to return the bird to its normal, cooler environment. Keep the bird in the warmed cage for at least two days, unless your veterinarian advises otherwise. Then gradually reduce the cage temperature to its normal level. This procedure often brings about immediate recovery.

In addition to supplying heat, try to encourage your pet to eat. If the bird has stopped eating, give it *anything* it will take and don't worry about a balanced diet. For example, if your pet likes peanut butter, oranges or corn on the cob, feed it as much of this favorite food as the bird will eat. A good emergency ration is turkey starter pureed with enough water to be fed from a dropper. Turkey starter, available from any feed store, is high in protein (27 to 30 percent) and contains all the essential nutrients needed by birds. Food given in this manner should be warmed to about 100 degrees Fahrenheit and care should be taken that the feed is actually saturated with water, not just wet. This will avoid digestive complications that would make an already bad situation worse. The next best thing to turkey starter is game bird starter. Honey and water fed from a dropper would help, too. If you can get your pet to eat *something*, it may mean the difference between life and death, so try.

Although you will become so attached to your pet that you will worry over every sneeze, try to resist the urge to medicate your bird unless it is prescribed by your veterinarian. Most avian ailments are difficult to diagnose because the symptoms of many diseases are similar. Accurate diagnosis by a trained professional who can provide the appropriate medicine in the correct dosage is the least your sick pet deserves. Do not administer petshop cures, including antibiotics, to save a veterinarian's fee. It may cost you your bird! Also, the practice of feeding antibiotics to a bird as a preventative measure is a serious mistake. You will only destroy the balance of natural bacteria in your bird's digestive system and end up with a truly sick bird. Rely on your good management and your veterinarian to prevent and treat disease!

MINOR PROBLEMS AND SIMPLE REMEDIES

If your bird is suffering from a minor discomfort, you can provide some simple remedies, listed below. However, first make reasonably certain that your bird is free of other symptoms. You would not want to delay treatment by your veterinarian of a possibly serious condition.

A note of caution is in order about the great number of products on the market for use with birds. You will find for sale inhalants, tonics, salves, ointments, feather-bathing sprays, insecticides in various forms and so on. Many of these products are useless and some can be harmful. When evaluating these products, consider the ingredients carefully. Oils or oil-based preparations should *never* be used because they will ruin the feathers' insulating properties, even when applied to unfeathered areas. Specific advice on some of these products is provided below. In general, spend caution—not money—and you will not go wrong!

Dirty Feet.   If your bird's feet are soiled from its droppings or sticky from handling fruit, first offer your pet a bath. If the bath fails to clean the feet, wash them yourself in lukewarm water or wipe them off gently with a moist soft cloth or cotton. Most tame birds will submit to this without making a fuss.

Scaly Feet and Legs.   The feet and legs of many types of birds, like canaries, have a scale-like appearance which is completely normal. As the bird ages, the scales may become thick and raised at the edge, resembling a tortoise's leg. This condition causes the bird no discomfort and is *not* a pathological problem. Treatment serves no purpose. Do not worry about it.

On the other hand, there is a mite that sometimes attacks the feet and legs (and also the beaks) of caged birds. It is commonly known as the "scaly-leg mite" and it produces a growth on the feet, legs, and sometimes the beak, that looks like concrete—foamy and irregular. If you suspect the presence of this mite, your veterinarian will be able to diagnose the condition and recommend treatment.

Blocked Nostril.   Occasionally, a bird will suffer a blocked nostril from a simple lack of humidity. You can provide quick relief by using a cold-water vaporizer or humidifier near the cage. Do not add inhalants (including those sold for use with birds) because they are irritating to the bird's delicate respiratory system. As the blockage loosens, wipe it away gently with a lukewarm water-soaked bit of cotton. If the condition does not clear up within a few days, seek your veterinarian's advice. A variety of mite or other problems may be responsible for the blockage.

Minor Eye Irritations. If a bird has been subjected to a draft or exposed to an infected bird, it might develop an eye irritation in one or both eyes. This would manifest itself in a "sticky" eyelid that won't open as usual or a watery eye. The bird will rub its eye on the perch and possibly infect the other eye as well. Don't delay treatment because a prolonged case could result in blindness.

The bird's eye(s) must be washed out twice a day. Any eyewash solution sold for human or animal use will serve the purpose. The use of ophthalmic ointments is not recommended, since the oil will ruin the feathers. An ideal eyewash for birds is Dacriose. It is available without a prescription from your pharmacist and squirts a fine stream when the bottle is squeezed. Just squirt enough to flush the discharge out of the bird's eye(s), then wipe it off the feathers. This method of application eliminates the risk of scratching the bird's cornea. If treatment does not result in rapid recovery, seek your veterinarian's advice.

Treating a bird's eye requires that you handle it bodily. A small bird that is a potential biter can be handled with gloves or a towel. Larger birds can be slipped into the mixing jar of a blender or other funnel-like container so that their heads are exposed and wings are restrained. With a very large bird, you will be better off if your veterinarian provides the treatment. Regardless of size, however, the bird will not like the treatment at all. You have no choice but to provide it. Let us hope that your untamed bird will forget it when the treatments are over. A tame bird will usually forgive you when it realizes you are providing relief.

Broken or Split Feathers. If your bird falls down or flies with force into an obstacle, it may bend or damage one or two feathers. This is a rare, almost freak, occurrence. Disheveled feathers do not require treatment; your bird will set them straight during its preening routine. However, if the feathers are broken and oozing blood, give your bird a few moments to relax and then pluck the damaged feathers. Take the feather in your hand and with a swift tug in the direction of growth, pull it out. A new feather will grow out within about six weeks. Get this operation over as quickly as possible, so your bird can settle down again in the privacy of its cage.

Overgrown Beak. Occasionally, a bird will develop an overgrown beak from lack of cuttlebone or chewing material, or from other reasons. Compared to other birds of the same species, an overgrown beak is fairly obvious. In the normal case, the upper and lower mandibles of hardbills and softbills meet at the point. The upper mandible of a hookbill is longer than the lower mandible, extending over by about one-third the total length (when closed). Although an overgrown beak is not at all painful to a bird, it can be deadly because the bird will not be able to crack seeds to eat. Therefore, overgrown beaks require immediate attention.

Have someone with experience trim the bird's beak, especially if you have a large bird. Otherwise, use a nail clipper and carefully trim the beak, little by little, into its normal contours. If you don't trim too much, the operation is painless—like cutting your fingernails. Afterwards, provide chewing material for your pet and teach it to use its cuttlebone or mineral block. Often, just scratching the surface of a cuttlebone with a nail file is enough to interest a bird into using it.

Mites and Lice.   Many varieties of mites and lice have been known to attack caged birds. The most frequently encountered are red mites and feather lice. Fortunately, none of these is especially common in pet birds.

Feather lice are small but visible to the naked eye. They lay their eggs along the shafts of feathers and eat their way across the feather in a line perpendicular to the shaft. You can detect their presence through simple observation or by examining shed feathers for their "tracks."

Mites are very tiny and will probably have reproduced to a large population by the time you detect them. They hide in cracks of wood, crevices and corners of the cage, and underneath cage paper. During the day their color is grayish. At night they come out of hiding and feast upon bird blood, turning red in their gorged state; thus the name "red mites."

If you suspect mites, you can detect them by covering the bird cage at night with a white or light-colored cloth while the room is still brightly lit. Then turn off the lights, wait an hour or two, turn on the lights, and remove the cloth. If mites are present, you will see them on the cloth, looking like specks of gray or red dust. (You can kill the little critters on the cloth by ironing it.)

Neither mites nor lice are cause for panic or shame. Anyone's bird can get them, and it is a relatively simple matter to eradicate them. There should not be any mites on your bird during the day, at least in theory, so remove the bird and attend to the cage first. Dip the cage into a receptacle of hot water and a disinfectant. A washtub or the bathtub will do. Any household disinfecting cleaner, including chlorine bleach, will serve the purpose. Soak the cage for a while, then scrub, rinse and allow it to dry. The same treatment should suffice for the perches, but it is probably safer to throw them away and use new ones. As a final measure, spray or dust the cage, perches and cage cover thoroughly with a mite-killing preparation (described below); let it dry and then return food and equipment to the cage. Then spray or dust the bird, too, and return it to the cage. Attend to the bird's play area with the same series of measures. After this initial treatment, spray or dust the cage, perches, cage cover and bird once a week for a while as a follow-up.

To kill lice, follow the same approach, but remember that follow-up treatments will be necessary as the lice eggs hatch.

Unfortunately, petshops stock many varieties of mite and lice killers in sprays, powders and solids that are labeled for use with birds but are toxic even when used according to directions! Carbaryl-based preparations (e.g., Sevin dust) are effective when used as directed and are readily available. Pyrethrin is the safest of all insecticides but does not always kill the insects. Some are merely stunned and fall off (which is helpful) and others are resistant to it. With an especially sensitive or valuable bird, it is worth a try. Ten percent malathion is also safe if used carefully. It is a very powerful insecticide and is used by many veterinarians and zoos to treat difficult insects like air sac mites. Because malathion is so strong, it should only be used if other, milder insecticides fail to control a problem. Malathion is available at a garden shop.

BIRD DISEASES AND YOU

If you own or acquire a parrot-like bird, you will probably hear un-informed people express alarm that you or members of your family may be inviting that dread and mysterious disease "parrot fever." Sometimes called psittacosis but more properly called ornithosis (parrots do not have a monopoly on the condition), it is an ailment seen in turkeys and street pigeons as well as hookbills. Birds with this disease usually have diarrhea, loss of appetite and some trouble breathing. If a human contracts this germ it is usually a flu-like disease which can develop into pneumonia. In humans and birds, the disease is responsive to antibiotics. If the disease is suspected, a physician and a veterinarian should be seen promptly.

What is the incidence of ornithosis? According to the Center for Disease Control in Atlanta, Georgia, 23 people contracted ornithosis in 1976, 33 in 1977 and over 100 in 1978. The growing incidence of ornithosis in humans parallels an increase in the pet bird population. However, compared to the number (in the millions) of caged birds in the United States, the incidence of human cases of ornithosis is, indeed, quite small.

Another important and highly contagious disease of birds is New-castle disease. Although it *very rarely* affects humans, it is very dangerous to poultry and is under careful scrutiny by the U.S. Department of Agriculture. The "Asiatic" form (or *velogenic viscerotropic* Newcastle disease) is endemic in wild and domesticated birds around the world and is the reason for the stringent quarantine procedures through which every bird that comes into this country legally must pass.

The likelihood of your contracting anything from your bird is truly remote unless you buy a "bargain bird" from a fly-by-night operator. Smuggling birds is big business—more profitable than smuggling drugs—and the ones that come in illegally have not gone through the quarantine stations set up to screen the problem birds. It is foolish to buy a bird that might have been smuggled; you are just asking for trouble. Stick to reputable pet dealers!

CHAPTER 5

Housing and Play Areas

A bird that is uncomfortable with any aspect of its care will not tame. So, it makes sense to choose its most important possession, the bird cage, with consideration of the occupant. I have witnessed many birds that were nervous in one cage calm down completely when transferred to a more suitable cage. A cage is not a passive influence on the bird; it matters. Equally important is what is in the cage and where it is placed. And, just as you would give thought to where your toddler will play, you must plan your pet's play area. It is no fun to play where nothing can be touched!

SELECTING A CAGE

In general, a pet bird's cage should meet the bird's basic space requirements, be sturdy enough to withstand the bird's beak power and be easy to clean. Your bird's space requirements depend on its size, wingspan and flight preferences. The cage should be large enough to accommodate your bird's height (and tail) and outstretched wings and enable it to turn around comfortably, if not fly. For a bird that will be allowed to fly, the larger the cage, the better.

The door of the cage should be large enough for the bird to pass through comfortably, without undue crouching. In general, a bottom-hinged door is best. When opened, it becomes a ramp for your pet to exit and enter the cage. A side-hinged door requires you to fasten it open; however, it is superior to a sliding door which always seems to slam shut —sometimes like a guillotine.

The perches used in the cage should conform to the size of your bird's feet. Ideally, the bird's feet should cover from one-half to two-thirds of the perch. If you provide more than one size or shape of perch in the cage, the bird's feet will be more relaxed. Although perches are usually round, they can be oval, square, rectangular or flat platforms. You can also substitute natural tree branches if you like.

Canary/large finch cage by Duett. Credit: Peter Sutherland.

Most commercially available bird cages correspond to these basic requirements, but some are better than others for certain kinds of birds. In all cases, however, choose a cage that will be easy to clean! This is more important than looks. (Your bird will beautify a plain cage by itself.) For example, round cages require that you cut out paper discs to line the floor. It is much more practical to buy a cage with a square or rectangular bottom. Spherical cages are the worst. Seed and droppings have nowhere to go except your floor in a cage of this shape. A wooden cage should not be used. A chewing bird could break out of it easily, and, more important, wood is a favored breeding ground for mites.

Standard budgie and canary cages are usually good for large finches, budgies, canaries and lovebirds, except for the floor-type variety (see illustration). These birds prefer to fly straight across, not up and down. A cage that offers flight space is much better than one that doesn't. Also, budgies and lovebirds get much of their exercise by climbing around the cage. A cage with a solid roof will restrict their fun.

Unless you can find a roomy budgie cage with an unusually large door, the standard budgie or canary cage is inappropriate for a cockatiel. Cockatiels require a roomier cage because of their length (about twelve inches) and large wingspan (about eighteen inches). A good bird store will stock a selection of suitable cockatiel cages. Otherwise, it would be better to buy a small parrot's cage for such a bird. It would be roomy,

Well-designed budgie cages by Hoei *of Japan.* Credit: Peter Sutherland.

A well-designed cage for small-to-medium-sized hookbills by Hoei of Japan. Because of wire-spacing, large door and deep seed cups, this model makes an ideal cockatiel cage. Credit: Peter Sutherland.

A typical floor-type cage by Crown. This type of cage can be used for small hookbills. It's roomy but provides no flight space. Credit: Peter Sutherland.

come with a large door, and be supplied with feed cups large enough to accommodate sunflower seeds. However, the perches would be too large and would need replacement.

Conures and small doves can be housed in small-to-medium parrot cages, depending on the length of the bird. Halfmoon Conures are often housed in budgie floor cages. Some owners prefer these because of the removable tops, allowing the bird to be released through the top or the door. If you use this type of cage, however, you will have to purchase large, hook-on feeders to accommodate the size of the feed. There is no floor space or flying room in a "floor" cage, so it should not be used for doves or pigeons.

For medium and large parrots as well as pigeons and doves the size of Ringnecks, a standard parrot cage is fine. However, before you purchase any cage for a parrot, imagine the bird sitting on the center perch. If your pet could not lean over and comfortably reach the front or back cage wires with its beak, the bird will feel insecure in the cage. In this case, a smaller cage is preferable, unless you can install extra perches to increase the bird's mobility. Sometimes, the direction of the cage wires on a parrot cage makes the installation of extra perches very difficult. Bear this in mind when shopping. Many parrot cages double as monkey cages, the only difference being the addition of a platform in one corner. This version of the parrot cage would be nice for a pigeon.

Macaws, except some of the "dwarf" varieties, need special cages. The standard large parrot cage does not accommodate the length of a full-sized macaw. (A Scarlet Macaw, for example, is three feet long.) Unfortunately, macaw-sized cages are hardly ever displayed. If you don't see such cages in a petshop, ask your pet dealer to show or describe large cages available from his suppliers' catalogs. Perhaps he can order the ideal cage for your pet macaw. If not, keep shopping. Many beautiful large cages are available by mail through the advertising pages of bird-oriented periodicals. (See "Suggested Reading.") If all else fails, you can convert a large, metal dog crate into a macaw cage by installing perches and feed cups.

Macaws and other large parrots are sometimes kept on open perches called "T-stands," and are secured to them by chains attached to their legs until they learn to stay put. This might seem like the ideal way to "house" a bird, but, in my opinion, it is one of the worst. Open perches restrict the bird's movement to an absolute minimum if the bird learns its lesson. And, if the bird is ever startled into flight, the leg chain would became a dangerous item. T-stands have their place, but I think it is much preferable to provide the bird with a cage. It provides exercise, privacy and security.

Special cages are available for mynahs. These cages resemble parrot cages, except that they are flatter. Mynah cages always come with two perches to enable the bird to hop back and forth across the cage. There

A typical, large parrot cage by Crown. Credit: Peter Sutherland.

This parrot cage by Prevue/Hendryx provides a little more head-room than the cage in the preceding illustration. The pull-out tray is galvanized to prevent rust—a real plus in any bird cage. Credit: Peter Sutherland.

A typical mynah cage by ReppCo. Credit: Peter Sutherland.

is a set of deflectors around the cage sides to keep food and other debris inside the cage, as well as a removable, sliding grill located between the cage itself and the floor. This grill keeps the bird off its droppings and away from fouled food that has dropped to the floor.

Cages for softbills should be selected on the basis of the general requirements noted above and, of course, the bird itself. A Pekin Robin needs plenty of flight space. A Shama Thrush needs clearance between the perches and the cage walls for its long tail.

There is no harm in buying your bird a deluxe cage, like a small parrot's cage providing two or three perching levels. But, during your taming period, it will be more difficult to coax your bird out of its deluxe accommodations. In fact, if you can afford the luxury of two cages, it would be better to house your bird in a small, utilitarian cage until it is tamed. Then you can give your pet a deluxe cage when you're sure it will come out. The spare cage could be used during periodic cleaning to house the bird or as a traveling cage if you have to take your pet to a veterinarian.

A spare cage is, in fact, recommended although getting one is optional. A simple box-type cage that does not provide actual flight space is best. You may never need it, but a spare cage will be very helpful under certain circumstances. Again, the spare cage can be used for travel and temporary shelter. It is usually easier to warm and keep warmed if first aid is necessary. Also, if you should need to administer medicine directly into the bird's beak or apply medication to a sore or injury over a period of days, you'll find it easier to catch the bird in a compact cage.

Depending on the size of your bird, there are many inexpensive animal containers that can be used for this purpose. I used a mouse cage for small birds by removing the exercise wheel and installing a perch and feed cups. Dog crates, which are sometimes collapsible, will serve medium to large birds. Show cages are also excellent.

OUTFITTING THE CAGE

Now that you have selected an appropriate cage (or replaced an inappropriate cage), try to keep it simple. The cage should represent primarily a feeding station and roosting location for your pet. Remove unnecessary perches permanently. Extra perches just catch the bird's droppings (which you want to avoid) and interfere with flight, stretching and wing-flapping space. Until your bird is tamed, remove swings, too.

If your parrot's cage comes with a removable floor grill, as do most parrot cages, I recommend that you remove it. Many parrots like to walk on their cage floors and some even roll around on their floors. In either case, allowing the bird to use the floor will promote exercise and provide foot relaxation from gripping the perch. If your bird should become ill and require first aid, you could reinsert the grill and use the gap between it and the floor for a heating pad.

It is a good idea to obtain a duplicate set of feed dishes when you first purchase your cage. Having extras on hand greatly simplifies cleaning. For example, you can serve your bird's water in a clean cup daily. The "dirty" cup is then washed along with your own dishes to use the next day. This system works for even the most forgetful.

If the seed cups that come with the cage are inadequate for the size of seed used, replace them. For lovebirds in budgie or canary cages, the little dishes sold to feed hamsters, mice and so forth are ideal. They are usually weighted to avoid tipping over and look like miniature dog dishes. These containers hold about one-half cup in liquid volume, about as much seed as is consumed by a lovebird in one or two days. Fill this cup with the lovebird's staple seed mix and place it on the floor, away from perches. This kind of dish can also be used for finches, canaries and budgies. A full dish will last two or three days. (Remember to blow away the seed husks daily.) The cage seed cup can then be used for gravel or as an extra water cup.

OTHER NECESSITIES

Also, get at least two extra, different looking feeding cups of the same style and color for treats. These dishes should be large enough to hold a wedge of apple. The treat cups, when used, will be attached to the cage in addition to the staple food cups.

For a small bird, you will also need a landing perch (unless the cage door is bottom-hinged, making a ramp entrance), so your pet will be able to hop out of its cage. More importantly, a landing perch will help your pet find the door when it's time to go back in. I think a bright color helps. Landing perches are sold in most petshops.

Your bird will also need a bathtub. Any shallow, not too slippery, flat-bottomed dish will do. A cake or pie pan is good for a small bird. An oblong baking dish or a roasting pan will work for a large bird. Bird tubs sold in petshops are okay, but your bird will enjoy the fun of a splashy bath in a larger container. Why buy something you already have? Hook-on bathtubs that attach to the cage door are frightening to some birds and are really too confining for the brave ones. These tubs, however, are better than no tub at all.

Until your bird is tamed, keep only one or two simple toys inside the cage. Since you don't want your bird to become attached to another bird, eliminate mirrors completely. Naturally, plastic bird companions will be taboo also. Even penguins should be regarded with suspicion. Bells, except the jingle-bell variety (which are sometimes toenail traps), rope toys and chew toys are examples of acceptable in-cage entertainment. Reserve ladders, pull-carts, ferris wheels and other more elaborate toys for your bird's play area.

An optional piece of equipment is a bird "playpen" or "playground." These are usually wooden or plastic trays equipped with a jungle-gym perch arrangement, a ladder and a swing. Some come with simple toys attached, too. Although you can improvise a playground yourself, the prefabricated ones offer a couple of advantages: they are easy to clean and portable.

You are going to be training your bird to use a certain area during its free time. If you use a playground, your bird will learn to attach itself to the playground itself rather than the location of the playground. The bird will eventually fly to it even if you suddenly place it in a different spot for one reason or another.

If you own a lovebird or a conure, you might want to buy it a nest box to sleep in. I've never tried this personally, but certain birds are said to prefer a nest box for roosting. If you get one, you'll never have to worry about nighttime drafts. The box will also provide daytime security and chewing entertainment. However, the bird will not use the nest box for sleeping unless it's attached high in the cage *above* perches. Provide litter material inside the box to facilitate cleaning.

Mynahs sometimes become accustomed to sleeping inside a paper bag or a cardboard shoebox. Presumably, these items are used because they are disposable. If you provide bags for your mynah, make sure the

This plastic and wire playground provides climbing space for a small hookbill. By Goldbug *of Japan.* Credit: Peter Sutherland.

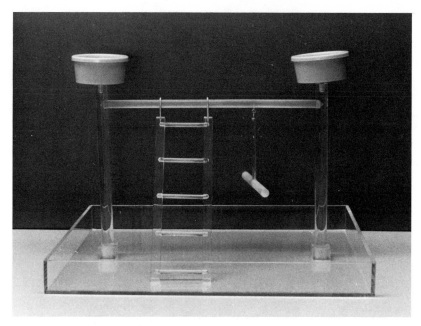

A clear Lucite playground for small hookbills. This Birds in Paradise *exclusive comes with a clear top and doubles as a cage.* Credit: Peter Sutherland.

A typical wooden playground for birds up to the size of cockatiels or conures, by Bob's Wood Products. *Canary "Dudley" Sutherland likes it, too!* Credit: Peter Sutherland.

A portable tabletop parrot perch, by Bob's Wood Products. Credit: Peter Sutherland.

A nifty sandbox perch for your giant macaw. From Birds in Paradise. Credit: Peter Sutherland.

size is large enough to enable the bird to turn around in it without getting stuck!

Your research will tell you whether the bird of your choice desires a sleeping container. If so, buy the style and size recommended for breeding.

CHOOSING YOUR PET'S CAGE AND PLAY LOCATIONS

The ideal location for your bird's cage will be bright, airy and close to the center of your activity. This spot should be a reasonable distance from windows, heaters, drafts and cooking odors. The distance should be at least six to eight feet, but, in the case of windows, about ten to twelve feet for southern or western exposures. Circulating air is not a draft: a direct continuous flow of air from a fan, an air conditioner, a forced air heating vent, is.

Although you may spend 50 percent of your time in the kitchen, this is a dangerous place. A dishpan filled with water, a hot running tap, excess heat, smoke and the stovetop might prove fatal to your bird sooner or later. Place the cage elsewhere to avoid calamities.

For convenience, you will want to locate the cage in or near the area in which your pet will be flying and playing. With parrots, heavy cages or floor-type cages, this is essential. With small birds in portable cages, you can carry the cage to another area, so it is not as important. However, if you locate the cage where your bird cannot see its play area, your pet will be more reluctant to come out of its cage when you move it. Your untamed pet will not want to abandon the security of its cage if it is not familiar with the play area. Therefore, it may take longer to begin active taming efforts.

The freedom area should be room-size or larger for a bird that will be flying. For a large bird, an area the size of a tabletop is adequate. Parrots usually don't fly; they require only stretching space. In any case, you will be able to increase your pet's play area once it's tamed by carrying it around with you.

This area must be safe for your free-flying pet. Besides obvious dangers, like open fans or hungry cats, open receptacles of water (like a goldfish bowl) pose threats to your pet. A canary belonging to a friend of mine met an undignified death by landing on a toilet seat, slipping into the bowl and drowning. Since then I have kept my toilet covered and the bathroom door closed.

A surprising number of popular houseplants (for example, dieffenbachia, schefflera, some philodendrons, etc.) are toxic to birds if eaten. If you know a plant to be poisonous, by all means remove it from your pet's play area. If you are unsure, it's better to be safe than sorry.

For the larger hookbills, I've found that including the floor in the play area is usually an invitation to disaster. From this vantage point, your bird will quickly discover valuable or dangerous objects, like furniture legs and electrical cords. My birds always discover any chrome around and "glue" themselves to the new-found bird—their own reflections. Supervision is not really the answer to the bird on the floor; discouragement is. Anything your parrot puts in its mouth is a toy and fair game as far as the bird is concerned. Trying to take away the toy, which could be the electrical cord, will not endear you to your pet. This action on your part is teasing—beware!

Finally, consider carefully which areas and furnishings in your home you want to protect from the bird. You don't want your budgie to mow down your prize African violets or your parrot to chew your antique rocker, so plan the freedom area thoughtfully. The room where your mynah or other softbilled pet will be flying should be easy to clean, particularly the floor. Your presence in this area during your pet's play time is vital to your taming efforts. Therefore, make sure it is a place where you will be willing to spend an hour or more every day without turning into a bird yourself! Your overall objective in selecting a cage and play location should be to control the bird's environment as much as possible.

PREPARING THE CAGE AND FREEDOM AREAS

Once you have selected these locations, you are ready to prepare the areas more or less permanently. You can then install the cage on a sturdy stand, high enough so that your bird can look around and feel secure, especially if you have a nosey dog free in the same area. Hanging a small cage from the ceiling by a chain or attaching it to the wall with a swinging plant hook are also acceptable installations. If you hang the cage, eye-level is about the best for ease of servicing.

To prepare the play area you will need a table or some kind of stand on which to place the playpen or simply toys, bathtub and goodies. For parrots, a parrot stand (or "T-stand" as they are sometimes called) is good. However, use the feeding cups only for treats. You want the bird to eat staple food inside the cage. Because you will have to pull up a chair next to the play station eventually, it will have to be high enough to accommodate you. A coffee table is not an acceptable surface; remember your bird prefers high to low. A card table or breakfast table is okay for a small bird. You can also use your own dining table, covered with a plastic tablecloth for protection and traction for the bird. A bird will not understand a clear, glass surface; it has to be covered.

When you are ready to release your bird, first secure the area. Close doors or darken areas where you don't want the bird to fly. Close un-

A heavy duty parrot T-stand. This stand is sold with a removable cage top.
Credit: Peter Sutherland.

screened windows and protect your uninitiated pet from the glass by lowering blinds or shades or by closing curtains. Your bird will regard the window as an invitation to the great outdoors. Try not to block out light; just provide the bird with an obvious barrier to the glass. If you have a large mirror in the room, you might want to cover it while your bird is flying around, too. Large mirrors give the impression that there is extra flying space inside. (I've almost walked into mirrors myself!) Remove valuables, other pets and whatever other dangers you might perceive. Plants known to be poisonous should be removed to another area permanently. Finally, if your chosen play area is not near the cage, take the cage to this location. Then fasten the door open, secure the landing perch and stand back.

CHAPTER 6

Establishing a Routine

Taming and, especially, training a bird require a consistent, systematic effort. You will get the most mileage out of your efforts if you establish a daily routine with your bird. Birds, like people, are creatures of habit. Take advantage of this fact.

Your most intense efforts to tame and train your bird will be during its free time, so you should choose this fixed daily hour with care. Your pet will be more receptive to taming and training at certain times during its day, as you'll learn in this chapter. Consider both your own daily schedule and your pet's routine. Your objective will then be to mesh them in the most convenient way. If you fail to establish a routine with your bird, especially a parrot, you may transform a lovable P-E-T into a tyrannical P-E-S-T, so this chapter is important.

YOUR SCHEDULE

First, consider your own routine. Determine a simple schedule of your usual activities from morning to night, Monday through Friday. Your weekends will probably be different, but for the purpose of planning for your bird, disregard them.

To illustrate the point, following are two examples of what might be typical schedules. Example A is a sample schedule of a person who is available at home during the day. Example B is a sample schedule of someone who is not.

Example A:
Typical Monday–Friday Schedule

7:30 A.M.	Arise, breakfast, etc.
9:00 A.M.	Shopping, busy
11:00 A.M.	Open

Noon	Lunch
1:30 P.M.	Errands, busy
3:00 P.M.	Open
5:00 P.M.	Prepare dinner, busy
7:30 P.M.	Open
11:00 P.M.	Retire

Example B:
Typical Monday–Friday Schedule

7:30 A.M.	Arise, breakfast, depart
9:00 A.M.–5:00 P.M.	Gone
5:30 P.M.	Return home, dinner
7:30 P.M.	Open
11:00 P.M.	Retire

Once you have established your typical schedule, determine when and for how long you will be available to the bird. In Example A, this person could use 11:00 A.M. to noon, 3:00 P.M. to 5:00 P.M., and 7:30 P.M. to 11:00 P.M. Owner B could use 7:30 P.M. to 11:00 P.M. for his or her bird.

YOUR BIRD'S ROUTINE

Now observe your bird's routine over a period of about three to four days. You will probably find that your pet is doing the same sorts of things at roughly the same times every day. Make a schedule for the bird, too. Again, two examples are provided of schedules prepared by Owner A and Owner B.

Bird of Owner A:
Typical Summer Schedule

7:30 A.M.	High activity: eating, chirping, hopping around, playing
1:00 P.M.	Preening
1:30 P.M.	Medium activity: eating, chirping, hopping around
3:00 P.M.	Sitting quietly
4:00 P.M.	Playing with toys
5:00 P.M.	Eating, chirping, hopping
8:30 P.M.	(sundown) Sleep

Bird of Owner B:
Typical Summer Schedule

7:30 A.M.	High activity: eating, making noise, wing-flapping, climbing around the cage
9:00 A.M.–5:00 P.M.	Unknown
5:30 P.M.	Eating
6:00 P.M.	Playing with toys, making noise
8:30 P.M.	(sundown) Sitting quietly, sleep

Note that the sample bird schedules above (which are completely fictitious) represent summertime hours, when daylight is longest. Although you will have the same schedule year-round, your bird will adjust its winter routine to squeeze whatever it does into a shorter day.

If you lengthen your pet's winter day by artificial lighting, which you surely will do for yourself, you run the risk of upsetting your pet's metabolism. This is a sorry note for those potential bird owners who live alone and leave for work in the morning and return at night in total darkness four to five months of the year! If this is your situation you might overcome this obstacle by purchasing an automatic lamp timer to carefully manipulate your pet's hours of "daylight" to coincide with your presence at home.

CHOOSING THE TAMING AND TRAINING HOUR

Now that you have established both your schedule and the bird's routine, you can choose its freedom hour. Periods of high activity are the most desirable times, followed by medium, then low, activity times. Your bird's preferred preening or privacy times are generally the poorest opportunities.

High activity times are best for taming and some forms of training because your bird will be most likely to play, fly, bathe and consume the goodies you offer. If you choose a nap time for freedom, your bird may head straight for a high roosting location, like the top of your drapes, and sleep for the entire hour. Your parrot might climb to the top of its cage and resent *any* advances. This would be annoying as well as boring for you.

In the examples, Owner A could devote 11:00 A.M. to noon to Bird A during its peak activity hours. This, then, would be the best choice. Owner B would have an hour, from 7:30 P.M. to 8:30 P.M., to devote to Bird B during a less active period.

Choose your taming and training hour accordingly. Then stick to this hour as much as possible, including weekends when you may have more time than usual. Naturally, you can give your pet treats and kind words anytime you want. Just reserve freedom for the specified hour.

When planning your pet's free time, don't plan a Monday-Wednesday-Friday arrangement. Your bird will not comprehend any schedule other than a daily schedule. If you own a bird capable of loud screeching (like a parrot) and you work, it might help to allow an adequate interval between the time you return home and the time you choose to work with your bird. If your pet is accustomed to waiting for you, it will be less likely to scream when you put your key in the door. In general, larger birds will be less adaptable to changes in routine than smaller birds. Once your pet is tamed, you can add extra free times to its schedule, but keep the routine principle in mind.

CHAPTER 7

General Taming Aids

Before you attempt to tame your bird, be reasonably certain that you understand bird behavior, that you are in control of your pet's environment—especially the play area—and that your chosen freedom hour is optimal in terms of your pet's habits and your schedule. I hope you will have learned as much as possible about your pet's species through research in other bird books. If you have accomplished these objectives, your taming efforts will succeed much more quickly.

A POSITIVE ATTITUDE

First, believe the fact that *you will be successful* in taming your bird. If you do not believe this, neither will your pet! I like to adopt the attitude that the bird is already tame—it just doesn't realize it yet—and treat it accordingly. Second, abandon any and all fears you may be harboring about your bird, especially with regard to biting. You *must* show ease and confidence when working with your pet. If you back away from your pet every time it approaches you, you will confuse and frustrate the bird. This is a promise: Your bird does not want to hurt you! Please believe this. Most birds *want to be tamed.* In my experience, the bigger the bird, the *more* it wants to be your friend.

Don't begin any taming attempts until you develop this confidence. You will have ample opportunity while your new pet is settling down, getting used to its new home and your presence. If you cannot settle down, perhaps you have acquired more bird than you can handle. There is nothing cowardly about such a conclusion. If so, you will be better off (and so will the bird) if you start with a smaller one.

SPECIAL CASES

You will be in an unusual taming situation if you have owned your bird for a number of years or have acquired an older bird that is not tame. These birds will have become more or less set in their ways. A bird that's

A Canadian businessman, the late Roy Ivor, feeds wild chickadees from his hand. These are only two of many wild birds that freely live on his bird reserve. Let this be your inspiration! Credit: Photo by Hugh Halliday, Courtesy of Carl Naether.

been in your home for a long time probably has developed a set of reactions to you, too. The taming program described in this Handbook will probably work just as well in your case as in the more typical case. A few preliminaries are suggested, however.

Of course, you will have to be *extra* patient at all times. Begin by trying to make a change in your pet's environment to help prepare it psychologically for the many other changes to come. A new cage or a new location for its present home are possibilities. Your objective is to slightly disorient the bird. At the same time, follow the other equipment guidelines described in this book. For example, remove mirrors and excess toys. Amend your feeding routine, if necessary. Prepare a play area, too. If you have a hookbilled bird, seriously consider wing-clipping, as described in the following section. This is not cruel; your bird will adjust rapidly. Finally, if there is a person in the home who dislikes the bird (and is probably disliked by the bird, too), minimize the contact between them.

As soon as you make these changes, select an hour to work with the bird every day. Then, begin taking the bird in its cage daily to your chosen play location, which should be set up as though the bird would be using it. For a week or two, just take the bird to this spot without opening the cage door. Your bird will then begin to realize that it now has two "special" places to be. If you won't be moving the bird, set up the play area adjacent to the cage so your pet can see and adjust to it.

Try to make the hour in the play area a special time for your pet. Provide treats only at this location, for instance, removing anything uneaten before returning the bird to its usual spot. After forty to fifty minutes, provide your usual in-cage bath container. When you think your pet has adjusted to the new routine, begin the taming process described in the following chapter.

If you have two birds housed in the same cage (except pairs of pigeons or doves or other compatible birds), you will have to separate them. Ideally, the birds should not even *hear* each other, so separate rooms are a must. You can, of course, try to tame both birds separately, but this will be time-consuming and probably wear thin your patience with them individually. I suggest that you select the bird that seems more receptive (less wild) or younger for taming and part with the other. At least, you might send it on a "vacation" for a few months with a friend or relative. Who knows, your neighbor might want to try to tame your extra bird! Once you are dealing with a solitary bird, follow the suggestions outlined above for the older bird.

WING-CLIPPING

Wing-clipping is a painless operation if performed properly—very much like cutting your hair—that discourages a bird from flying. The method recommended here is to clip the primary flight feathers on one wing, using the primary coverts as a guide. See the illustration showing the proper cutting line. If you clip too close, you will cut into the live, blood-charged portion of the feather quills, causing both pain and likely feather troubles (i.e., ingrown feathers).

Only one wing is clipped so that when the bird attempts to fly, one wing is more powerful than the other. As a result, the bird will aim for one point and fly circularly toward another. When the bird discovers that it can't reach its destination, it will usually stop trying.

If both wings are clipped, the bird will retain equal power in both wings and will be able to fly straight to its target. However, flight will demand much more exertion so this pattern of clipping serves effectively to slow down, not stop, flight. This clipping pattern is usually recommended for an overly aggressive bird. It is also possible to clip all but the first three, primary flight feathers on both wings. This clipping pattern slows down the bird while maintaining its neat appearance.

When the bird next molts the clipped feathers will be shed to be replaced by new growth. Only a few primary flight feathers are required for flying, so watch your bird and reclip when and if necessary.

Wing-clipping is a taming aid *only* because it forces a bird to remain where you put it. Thus you have better control over the bird. It also forces the bird to depend on you for protection and mobility; however, you will have to convince the bird of this new dimension in your relationship during your taming effort. *Wing-clipping is not a magical formula to ensure taming success!* You will have to earn your pet's confidence in order to tame it, whether or not you clip its wing.

Wing-clipping is an option for hookbilled birds only. It is not necessary for some hookbills, however, and not recommended for others. With the exception of the larger parrots, wing-clipping is neither necessary nor desirable for a young bird that has been handfed or that was handled by the breeder while still in the nest. These birds will be already tame or extremely receptive to taming and training. Young budgies and cockatiels, as well as lovebirds (when acquired directly from the nest), do not require wing-clipping either, since they are usually receptive to taming. Hardbills and softbills, with the possible exception of mynahs, should *never* be clipped because of their size, temperament and feather structure. Recall, these birds are not "climbers." If you clip the wing of such a bird, how will it maneuver about its cage?

Wing-clipping is recommended for conures and parrot-sized birds in general. After the taming period, however, conures and small parrots (for example, Senegals, Caiques, members of the *Pionus* family and small Amazons) should be allowed to feather out for eventual flying, unless the bird would not be manageable otherwise. The decision whether your small parrot should fly for exercise should be determined, I think,

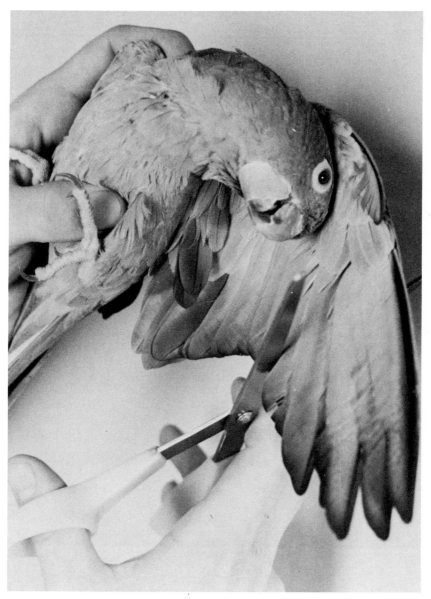

"Frodo" Cigala poses to demonstrate wing-clipping. Only the long, primary flights are cut. Unfortunately, the feathers to use as a cutting guideline are on the other (not shown) side of the wing. Credit: Peter Sutherland.

on an individual basis. As long as you can control the bird, the bird will be better off if it can fly. Large parrots should remain clipped permanently. These birds usually do not attempt to fly anyway, since the act of flying demands so much exertion and take-off space. But, if startled, a large, heavy-bodied bird *will* attempt flight with potentially disastrous results. It could fly into a window or other obstacle and break its neck. A large bird with flight capabilities also possesses a large beak and the mobility to exercise its destructive powers. It is possible to clip the wing but impossible to control the beak!

Wing-clipping will also help subdue an unusually aggressive hook-bill, regardless of its size, so it is recommended in this case. In addition, wing-clipping is always an option in the case of a bird that shows continued resistance to your taming efforts or in the case of a bird where all other management efforts have failed. For example, an older budgie or cockatiel that continues to fly to inaccessible locations during its free time and cannot be persuaded to return through less drastic methods should be clipped.

Clipping a wing should not prevent a bird from breaking the impact of a minor fall. However, a bird whose wing is clipped is left completely defenseless. If your bird is clipped, be very careful to protect it from predators, like dogs, cats and human feet.

When you first get your bird, have the seller clip its wing, if necessary; watch how it's done so you will be able to perform the operation yourself. If you are buying a young budgie or cockatiel, ask the seller to show you where to cut, in the event you should decide to do so later.

Keep in mind that even a clipped bird will attempt to fly away if it is frightened. During your taming sessions, this is bound to happen at least once. So, be careful to safeguard the area from other pets as well as dangers that you might not remove otherwise. For the first few aggressive taming attempts, carpet the area around the bird's play station to soften potential falls.

NOTE: In the following chapter, all parrots will be assumed clipped and incapable of flight.

FOOD

Food "extras" are valuable taming aids, so definitely use them. If you do, you are sure to succeed at taming much more quickly than otherwise. If you have ever seen trained animal acts, perhaps you have noticed the trainer reward the animal with a tidbit. Food is a very powerful device!

Offer a variety right from the start to determine what your pet likes as well as to teach it to accept new and different foods. Food provides another example of the advantage of taming young birds rather than old birds. The young ones will be more likely to try new foods, so you would have more ammunition in your taming arsenal. But, young or old, every bird will accept at least *one* of the many suggested food extras (see Chapter 3). Don't be discouraged if your pet shows little or no interest in your treats; keep trying.

Most hardbills love leafy greens almost immediately. Softbills and hardbills that are given the chance love oranges (sliced at the end to expose a small part of each section), apples, other fruit and corn on the cob. Naturally, serve bird-sized portions, such as a wedge of apple (peeled). If you slice each row of corn down the center with a knife, even the tiniest hardbill will be able to enjoy it. Most finches and almost all softbills accept mealworms (and other live food) greedily. If yours likes mealworms and you don't mind handling the squirmy things, offer a worm directly from your fingers. The bird will probably take it. As soon as your small bird shows a strong liking for a treat, coax it to eat while you hold the treat. If the bird is tiny enough, next try to get the bird to sit in your hand to eat the tidbit. No canary worth its song will pass up a spinach leaf, even if you're on the other end. And, so it goes with softbills and mealworms.

For conures and parrots, which can hold onto treats with their feet, offer extras *directly*, as soon as the bird is settled and shows no fear when you are nearby (a condition described in the next chapter). In addition to fruit and leafy greens, most parrots readily accept peanuts, shelled nuts, and dog biscuits (sized according to bird). Grapes, cherries, berries and fresh peas are also good, bite-sized treats. Since parrots can hold their food, try small celery and carrot sticks, too. Always offer your parrot a portion it will be able to hold and once it latches on to the treat, let go. If you continue to hold the treat, your parrot may interpret it as teasing. Of course, you cannot allow anyone to tease your pet. The fact that the bird takes a treat directly from you will be your taming advantage.

Besides making your pet healthier and happier, food extras can be used to help manage and control your bird. For example, a piece of lettuce or fruit, strategically placed, will persuade the most reluctant bird to come out of its cage. Right on the landing perch or in clear view outside the cage are ideal spots to place your delicious bribes. By the same method, you can persuade your reluctant friend to return to its cage. Show the bird the favored morsel, then place it just inside the cage in clear view or on the landing perch. When the bird flies to the bait, close the door. Whenever you need help managing your pet, try food first. It's painless and your bird's confidence in you will increase with every bite.

TOYS

Toys are not as direct as food in helping to tame your bird, but they are valuable and should be provided. Toys will entertain and stimulate your pet to exercise for hours, give you better control over the bird and dis-

Place a treat on the landing perch to coax your shy pet to come out of the cage or to return to it. Credit: Peter Sutherland.

courage destruction of your property. A parrot with chew toys, for example, cannot scream and chew at the same time and will be less likely to crave your woodwork. These toys need not be store-bought; your bird will not know the difference nor will it care.

Not all birds will play with toys, however, and even those that do may regard a strange, new toy with suspicion for several days. Hardbills and small softbills are the least likely to take naturally to toys, although they will use a bird playpen. Hardbills particularly appreciate the playpen if its tray is filled with gravel. Try simple toys, like bells and ladders, for these birds. They will get most of their exercise through flight, so don't be concerned if these birds ignore even simple toys.

Hookbilled birds usually love toys and will spend hours destroying them. Wrecking the toy is the bird's pleasurable objective, so don't be dismayed or surprised by it. Just replace them; bird toys are inexpensive.

Small hookbills, like budgies, lovebirds and cockatiels, and mynahs will accept most of the bird toys sold in petshops. These birds will not be able to destroy plastic toys, so you can use them safely. Do provide chew toys; they don't last long, but small hookbills need and love to chew. These birds will use and appreciate bird playpens, too. They are nominal in cost and will help you contain potential messes.

Big-beaked hookbills require sturdy toys. Plastic toys made for small birds should not be used. Your bird will destroy a plastic toy very quickly and may swallow the sharp, indigestible pieces. Unfortunately, parrot-strength toys are not offered by every petshop, but this is gradually changing. Even parrot-sized playpens are beginning to appear. At any rate, with a little imagination it is easy to make or buy suitable toys. For example, a parrot fancier from Pittsburgh provides an ingenious play area by installing a large tree branch in a Christmas tree holder. Presto, an indoor tree!

Dog toys, like rawhide chew toys, small wooden dumbbells (sold for dog obedience training) and latex squeaky toys, are good parrot pacifiers. Other good, improvised toys include: a length of chain (attached inside or outside the cage for climbing), a key ring with colorful blank or no-longer-used keys, baby spoons (yummy when filled with peanut butter), wood clothespins and wood scraps. (Parrots enjoy peeling the bark off tree branches. However, do not provide leaves, and avoid evergreens.)

You can make your parrot an interesting toy by stringing bells and a couple of simple toys (like a rawhide shoe or hat, a wood spool, a measuring spoon) on a leather shoelace. Just knot the shoelace, string on a toy, knot again, skip a few inches, knot the shoelace, string on a toy, knot again, and so on. Then attach it securely to the cage top so that it dangles near a perch.

If you want to give your tame parrot a mirror, use stainless steel rather than glass. A parrot will eventually break a glass mirror and may

A *display of perches and toys at* Birds in Paradise. Credit: Peter Sutherland.

This Lucite hanging perch makes a nice rest stop for your small flying buddy. A Birds in Paradise *exclusive.* Credit: Peter Sutherland.

injure itself on the debris. Anything within your parrot's reach will be considered a toy by the bird. Therefore, remove dangling earrings, diamond rings, necklaces, watches and other such articles before your pet does!

A few simple cautions about toys are in order. Steer clear of toys with small crevices which might trap your bird's toenails: jingle bells, small link chains, etc. Also avoid toys shaped like small nooses, such as some plastic ring toys. Don't provide cloth toys which the bird might unravel. Never use thread to hang toys, because your bird might become tangled in it. (It is no picnic trying to unravel tightly wrapped string from a parrot's toes!)

FREEDOM

Every time your bird emerges and returns to its cage, it will learn that you are not a threat. Thus, you will be winning your pet's confidence daily if you provide freedom. Freedom, of course, is necessary if your bird is to play with toys, accept your treats and take a decent bath.

On a practical level, freedom is essential to taming because your bird must learn to trust you and come to you. The bird can't do this trapped in a cage! It is a very rare bird, indeed, that doesn't come to regard its cage as its own private castle. Such a bird would bitterly resent an intrusion as aggressive as hand-training in its home. Besides this, try putting your hand through the door of a typical bird cage, then try to imagine how you will remove your hand with a bird perched on it. With most cages, this is a physical impossibility.

One final point: In no sense do I mean to equate freedom from the cage with freedom to roam unsupervised. You do your pet no kindness to allow it freedom from its cage while you are away. A budgie, canary or other little bird will probably be okay unsupervised while you run down to the corner store for milk. But the ordinary household abounds in potential dangers which might do in your pet in the five minutes of your absence. Be careful.

A large hookbill, on the other hand, should never be left unsupervised. A parrot has no sense of property value. Your plasterboard walls are just as good as cuttlebone. Wallpaper is just as much fun to peel off the wall as is bark from a tree branch. The piano leg is just a different-shaped bone to chew. And so on. Besides your property, the bird's own safety is at stake. I read a report of lead poisoning in an unsupervised parrot that chewed the lead weights out of a drapery hem. Danger truly lurks in odd places for the unsupervised pet.

COMPANIONSHIP

A pet bird is a social animal removed from its own kind. You are therefore obligated to act as its companion. Don't underestimate your bird's desire for company and your ability to provide it. Even if the bird shows no immediate pleasure in your presence, it will eventually. This is what taming is all about, after all.

PATIENCE

Wing-clipping, treats, toys and freedom will go a long way in helping to tame your bird, but in the end, your PATIENCE will finally do the job. *Never lose it!*

CHAPTER 8

The Business of Taming and Training

Now you are ready to get down to the serious business of taming and training. This chapter describes a progressive taming and training effort, divided into six stages. Because taming, particularly, is a continuous *process*, the borders between stages are rather fuzzy. It is not necessary to follow the taming method outlined here verbatim. You can improvise according to your pet's temperament and its reaction to taming and training. There is no *one* taming method, except *patience*.

During the bird's taming, be gently aggressive. No one can estimate how long each stage will take. Your bird will more or less show you, through its behavior, when it is ready for the next step. Be careful not to miss your cues.

STAGE 1: GETTING SETTLED

Depending on your bird, it will require anywhere from two hours to two weeks or more to settle itself in its strange, new surroundings. Give your new pet as much time as it needs. As a minimum standard, it must be able to: find and feel comfortable on its perches, maneuver easily around the cage and feel unthreatened enough to eat in your presence. Don't do anything else unless your bird shows you that it can do each and every point mentioned.

If your new bird was handfed or is very young, it will probably settle down in its cage very quickly. Give these birds a couple of days to adjust anyway. Birds that are immature (but not acquired directly from the nest) and parrots will probably need more time. It will vary according to individual bird.

Your settling-down time is not wasted time. There is much to accomplish. Use this time to observe your bird from a polite distance. Try to determine your pet's disposition. Observe whether it plays with the toys provided. Begin feeding food extras immediately (just place extras in a treat cup for now) and try to determine your pet's tastes, so you can use its favorites to tempt it in following stages. Finally, when the bird seems somewhat adjusted, observe its routine over at least three or four days. Continue to observe your bird's behavior into the next taming stages. It will help you predict its reactions to your advances.

During this settling period, treat your bird like an honored guest. Approach its cage often and talk to the bird in a reassuring voice. Tell it your troubles if you want, but do it reassuringly. Play pleasant music on the radio so that your pet will become accustomed to humanity. However, while your bird is settling down, protect it from too much humanity, like abrupt motions, any waving of the arms, children who might poke their fingers into the cage, or shouting. Your calm behavior will do much to settle your new pet quickly.

As soon as your pet seems settled, go on to Stage 2. However, if you have an extremely active bird, like a Pekin Robin or a small finch, I recommend that you begin the feeding part of Stage 3 *in the cage.* That is, get the bird to accept food from your hand as soon as the bird seems settled. You will need to develop the beginnings of a pet relationship with such a bird *before* you provide freedom, so that the situation will be manageable. You will *never* catch a Pekin Robin, for example, unless it will pay attention to you. This treatment is not necessary with a mynah, but it would be helpful.

If you have a very nervous bird, I suggest you follow the instructions provided in the preceding chapter for older birds. That is, take the bird in its cage to the play area for its daily play hour, but do not open the cage door for a few days. Then the bird will not be totally surprised when you eventually offer freedom in this spot.

STAGE 2: FREEDOM

When your bird appears to be ready for freedom, make sure that *you* are ready. Your bird's play station should be prepared, the area must be secured (don't forget to cover windows and large mirrors!) and you should have at least one favored treat on hand to help you control the bird, just in case. If you lose control of the freedom situation, don't become impatient or forget the basics you have studied so far. If you should resort to chasing, for instance, you will find yourself at square one again. So, feel prepared and confident before you begin.

When you release your bird for the first time, the chances of its actually coming out are only fifty-fifty. If your pet doesn't step out immediately, don't force it. Once you open the cage door, seat yourself at a comfortable distance (from the bird's point of view) and give your pet at least forty minutes to emerge. Even if the bird doesn't come out, it will

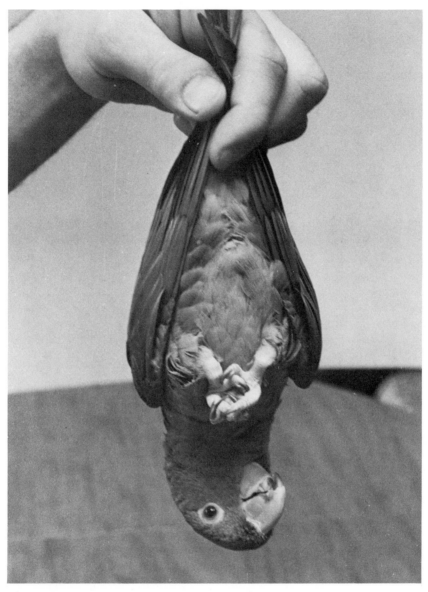

This level of trust does not happen overnight! Give your bird and yourself plenty of time. Frodo, a White-Eyed Conure, is the well-trained pet of Glenn Cigala, College Point, NY. (Frodo is also a stunt bird; do not attempt this trick with your pet.) Credit: Peter Sutherland.

probably display some interest in the new situation—an open door and an inviting array of goodies outside. After about forty minutes, close the cage door and return the cage to its location, if it has been moved. Try again the following day. Regardless of how long it takes, *never* force your bird out of the cage!

If your pet doesn't want to come out after a few days, try using a decoy, like a ceramic bird or a Christmas ornament of a bird figure. Just place the decoy outside the cage where your pet can see it. If your pet responds to the decoy, keep using it for a few days, then eliminate it. The bird will develop the habit of leaving the cage and will do so even when the stimulus (the decoy) is long gone.

If your bird is extremely shy and resists freedom for an unreasonable amount of time, say two or three weeks, try gentle pressure tactics. One method is to remove all the bird's perches and replace them with a single perch that extends out the cage door. The bird will then get onto the only perch in the cage and eventually move along it to the outside. In most cases, it will then climb up to the cage top. Another form of pressure, if the bird likes toys, is to remove all toys from the cage and place them on the play surface. You can also remove the bird's food dishes, placing them outside the cage. Of course, you must put them back in two or three hours whether or not you're successful in luring the bird to come out.

All these pressure tactics will probably require more than an hour of patient waiting on your part, so don't use them unless you have plenty of time. Once the bird finally emerges, you must make the experience painless! Leave the bird alone for at least forty minutes. Then, calmly, slowly, and speaking reassuringly, return food dishes and perches, if removed, to the cage. Remove yourself again and wait for the bird to step willingly back into the cage. This could take a few hours. It's important for the bird to realize that coming out of the cage is not scary or dangerous. So, again, don't try any pressure techniques unless you have the time to wait for your very timid friend to emerge and return to the cage without any additional interferences by you. After one or two of these sessions, the bird will learn that freedom is not only painless but enjoyable. Then it will come out without any scheming on your part.

If the bird steps out the first time, wonderful. Don't interfere with it in any way. Everything should be ready in advance. It will probably fly awkwardly around the room or head straight for the top of the cage if its wing is clipped. Keep your eye on it to protect it from unforeseen dangers. Its flying skills will improve with practice and greater familiarity with the layout of the land.

After about twenty minutes, if the bird returns to the cage, shut the door and end the free time early. The bird will have learned its first lesson. Otherwise, after about thirty to forty minutes of play time, begin your attempt to return the bird to its cage. If you start at this point, you will have twenty to thirty minutes in which to accomplish this, so don't rush or display impatience.

If the bird is not within sight of the cage, corral it into the area by approaching the bird slowly. Whistle or talk softly as you approach to help calm the bird. As soon as you get near, the bird should fly out of the area—let us hope into an area where it can see the cage. Then show your bird a favored treat, place it on the landing perch or conspicuously inside the cage, and move out of the way. Give the bird a reasonable amount of time to go for the treat before you try another method. If it flies away while you're waiting, approach your pet again so it will return to the cage area. This method almost always works. Be sure to give it a chance.

If the bird repeatedly refuses to return to its cage, try returning the cage to its usual location. Perhaps the bird will feel more comfortable returning to its customary spot in the beginning. Even if your appointed hour is over at this point, your bird will have to return to the cage for food. Don't become frenzied.

As a last resort, you can return a bird to its cage by darkening the room. Turn off all lights, draw the shades and approach the bird. In a steady motion, gently grasp the bird bodily and place it on the floor of its cage. Then restore the lights. If the bird is a potential biter, use a bath towel to pick it up. In the dark, the bird does not know what is happening, so having done this, your future relationship will not be harmed.

The first time your clipped parrot steps out of its cage, it will probably head straight for the top of its cage and flap its wings vigorously. This is desirable exercise and cage tops are part of the play area. You may even want to wire a perch or branch permanently to the cage top for your bird's comfort and chewing pleasure. Eventually, the bird will come down to investigate the play surface. Seat yourself well back from the cage and just observe. When the bird returns to the cage for food, shut the door.

If the parrot jumps down from its play surface for any reason, place the cage on the floor next to the play table or stand. Then corral the bird back to the cage, speaking softly. Most likely, it will climb onto the cage immediately. Whether the bird will return on its own to the play surface is uncertain. If not, just pick up the cage, bird and all, and return it to its place. If the bird jumps down again, repeat the process. This method has never failed for me.

While on the subject of returning a bird to its cage, let me offer a couple of suggestions regarding the tame pet. Eventually, you will be able to just pick up your bird (on your finger, *not* bodily) and return it to the cage. But, often the bird would rather not enter the cage. Hookbills, in particular, tend to grab onto the frame of the open cage door and pull themselves up to the cage top. This behavior and your resulting exasperation can be avoided by placing your free hand above the bird's back as you near the cage. This will inhibit flight. When you arrive at the cage, move your free hand, still hovering over the bird's back, so that the side of your hand rests against the top frame of the cage door. Having done this, you cover any cage wires the bird might latch onto and block its path to the cage top. Then, put the bird on a perch inside the cage. You will get better at this technique with practice.

If getting your tame pet back into its cage becomes a problem, try saving its edible goodies as rewards for going home, whether or not a struggle has ensued.

Returning to Stage 2, continue providing freedom daily. As the bird appears calmer in your presence, move closer and closer to the play area, day by day. Then proceed to Stage 3.

STAGE 3: FOOD AND BATHING

At this point, do not provide treats automatically at your bird's play site. Wait until the bird steps out and offer food directly. If the bird will not accept food immediately from your hand, then place the treat on the play surface as usual. Keep trying. If, after a few days, the bird still does not accept the food from your hand, hold it steady a few inches away but within easy reach for a minute or two. Then take it away. If the bird is indisposed to accept it fairly soon, it will probably not do so after a long wait, either. Return in five minutes and try again. Avoid giving the bird the feeling that it is being threatened by the proximity of your hand. Sooner or later, the bird will not be able to resist your offer.

This is also a good time to introduce the bath outside the cage. After about thirty minutes of free time, bring your bird's tub to the play station. Most hardbills and softbills do not need any encouragement to bathe. However, hookbills often do. If so, try placing a leafy green in the water, half in, half out, and move away. This may persuade your pet to investigate. Another method is to place a small mirror, face up, in the tub. A bird will get into the water to see the "other" bird. As soon as your pet learns the purpose of the tub, however, remove the mirror permanently. Don't be concerned if your bird doesn't seem to understand. In a few days, it will take a drink (to test the water temperature and depth) and step in. Once your bird steps in, it needs no further assistance. Provide the bath every day, depending on the weather indoors.

If your parrot repeatedly refuses a bath, keep providing the tub, but also test the spray or sprinkle methods. Spray above the bird, so the mist falls on your pet from above like rain. Sprinkle from above also, except be sure not to wildly shake your sprinkling device. If you scare the bird, you won't know if it objects to the water or your application.

If the parrot likes the spray or sprinkle, it will extend its wings and perhaps even turn on the perch to catch more of the drops. It may also screech with delight. If the bird doesn't like this bathing method, it will probably jump off its perch and head back to the cage to get away. If so, keep trying every other day or so until the bird accepts it or shows clearly that it hates the bath routine. A parrot is very long-lived; you will have plenty of time to teach it to bathe. Don't rush the bird.

After your pet has accepted food offered directly from your hand, proceed to Stage 4. A little bird is ready for the next stage when it will consume food that you are holding. If it will stand on your hand to eat, skip the stick-training steps outlined in the next section.

STAGE 4: HAND-TRAINING

At this point, your bird is partially tamed. This is when you should be prepared if the bird approaches you first—lands on you or steps onto your shoulder or arm. This can and does occur quite often; so don't be surprised, be delighted, if your pet makes the first aggressive move. A bird that flies can approach you from any point, but a clipped bird requires an opportunity. You can provide one by seating yourself next to your pet's play station. In either case, once it's on you, don't move at all. You don't want to alarm your pet. Instead, say something like, "Oh, what a brave bird you are!" The bird will probably fly away immediately and return one or more times. Leave it up to the bird. In the case of a parrot, *don't panic*. A bird that willingly steps on your shoulder will *not* bite you. It might nibble affectionately on your hair or your ear. You must give it a chance to show you its gentleness. At any rate, limit your motion to soft words or whistling.

If you are sitting and the bird remains on your shoulder and seems to be at ease, while preening your hair or gently nibbling on your shirt, slowly raise your arm nearest to the bird and rest it on the play surface. Hopefully, it will walk onto your arm. Once your pet is on your arm, you should have little or no trouble getting it back on in future attempts. If you get this far, skip entirely the stick-training steps outlined below; use your arm instead.

If your bird does not approach you on its own, it should trust you enough at this stage not to run or fly away when you approach its play surface. If so, it is time to offer your pet a perch. If you and the bird seem to be ready, *it is always preferable to use your finger, hand or arm immediately instead of a wooden perch.* Use the same approach described in the following paragraphs, except substitute "hand" for "stick." If this proves unsuccessful, *then* try a wooden perch. Also, do *not* wear gloves, wrap a towel around your arm or go out of your way to wear long sleeves. Long sleeves, by the way, are usually slippery for the bird. This is un-

Spotty, the talking pet budgie of Joe Marssdorf (shown here), says, "Who needs a perch? These eyeglasses are just fine." Credit: Peter Sutherland.

necessary and will create an obstacle in your relationship. If you are tempted to resort to this sort of protection, *you* are not yet ready for hand-training. Wait a while longer until you build up your confidence!

To train the bird, hold the stick steady (horizontally, of course) directly in front of the bird at the level of its thighs. Speaking softly, invite it onto the stick. Try offering one of its favorite treats as an enticement. If necessary, gently nudge your pet with the stick. This tends to throw the bird off balance so it will instinctively step up. If it steps on, don't move the perch. Some birds will meet you halfway by putting only one foot on the stick. This is acceptable progress. Don't force the issue! The bird will get on with both feet soon enough, perhaps next time. Continue to speak softly to the bird and allow it to take or nibble on the treat. If the bird remains with both feet on the perch (and has eaten the tidbit) *very slowly* move the stick. Most birds will jump off at this point, realizing that this is no ordinary perch; it moves! Give the bird a few minutes to rest and start again at the beginning.

If your pet does not step on the stick, try offering it again in a few minutes. Restrict your attempts to three or four per session so that you don't annoy the bird and risk losing some or all of its confidence. Eventually, the bird will step on or approach you on its own.

After the bird steps onto the stick, you should begin your efforts to eliminate it by coaxing the bird onto your hand instead. This can be accomplished in a short time by gradually reducing the length of the stick. You can either use a physically shorter perch or you can try grasping the existing perch in the center, giving the bird a shorter length on which to climb. Hold the stick steady until the bird shows it is calm. Then move it slowly. Walk around the play station. Then deposit your pet back on the play surface. Do this again in five to ten minutes.

During the next session, offer an even shorter length of stick. After the bird steps on, try slowly dipping the end of the stick where the bird is sitting lower than your hand. This may persuade the bird to sidestep directly onto your finger or hand. If you succeed, nonchalantly remove the perch with your other hand and *don't move*. Other than dipping your hand, you might try nudging the bird sideways by slowly placing a finger at the end of the stick. To get away from this finger, the bird may step on your other finger or hand.

Regardless of methods, once the bird is on your hand for the first time, don't move. The bird will quickly realize where it is. Speak softly or whistle. With your other hand, offer the bird a treat. If the bird remains, slowly move your hand. A few minutes later, offer your hand directly to the bird to reinforce the lesson.

Once the bird has been on your hand a couple of times, eliminate the stick entirely. Otherwise, there will always be something between you, stunting the potential of your relationship. Offer your hand directly

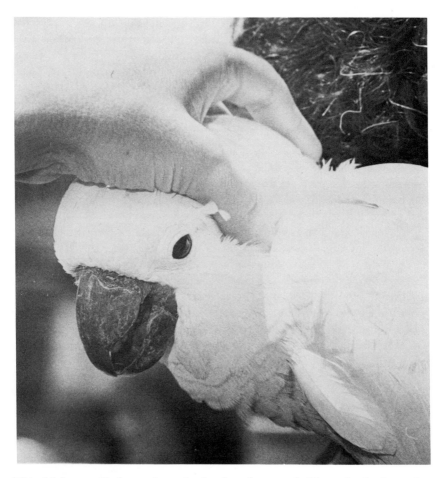

This Moluccan Cockatoo bows its head to be petted. Note the beak in the closed position, showing the bird's tongue. Credit: Jean M. Hawthorne.

to the bird. Try to get the bird to step from one hand to the other or from one finger to another, like a ladder. Let the bird walk up your arm to your shoulder, so that it can investigate your hair.

STAGE 5: BECOMING MORE INTIMATE

At this stage, your pet is thoroughly hand-trained. Now is the time to introduce your bird to others as well as to strengthen your bond with the bird.

If your bird is a hookbill, try gently scratching its head. Many budgies will not allow this, but most cockatiels and parrots love it. You'll never know if your bird likes it unless you try. You can approach head-scratching nonchalantly by gently stroking your bird's chest while it is perched on your finger. Then work your way up slowly to the bird's "cheeks." Once at cheek level, try scratching. This should be done in the direction of the bird's feathers, with a gentle, zig-zagging motion of the fingers. Since you will not be using your fingernails, this is not really scratching. Be careful not to bend any feathers backwards or break pin feathers (feathers that are just beginning to grow out and are encased in a sheath).

If your bird likes being scratched, it will probably bow its head and perhaps ruffle its feathers to encourage you to continue. Scratch the top of its head and neck. Many parrots like to be scratched under the wings. These birds will lift a wing to help you along. Once a bird shows a liking for being scratched, look out! Your pet will "beg" you to scratch it often. Some birds will even take hold of your finger to bring it up to their heads. Most of them will bow their heads the instant they see you.

Use whatever method works best for you in attempting to scratch your pet's head, but remember that your bird will probably recoil if you reach from above (at least, at first). If you have no luck with your attempts to scratch the bird, try taking it into an unfamiliar room. Birds will usually allow more intimacy in a strange place where *you* are the only familiar object. Scratching can then lead to bodily petting and eventually to complete handling with some birds. Try kissing, too. Hopefully, your pet will ever-so-gently nibble your lip.

Some hardbills and softbills and most hookbills that like to be scratched will allow you to pet them. You would approach this in the same manner as scratching. Begin on the chest where the bird can see what you're doing and realize you mean it no harm. If your bird does not object to your stroking its chest, then gradually move to its back. A bird that likes to be petted can be taught to "play dead" or to stand on its head as you gradually become more aggressive with petting.

Tame birds, particularly parrots, may show definite preferences for certain people. Parrots are usually regarded as one-person birds. Your

Pablo and Frodo (Blue and Gold Macaw and White-Eyed Conure) lie in owner/ trainer Glenn Cigala's hands while Frodo keeps a cautious eye on Pablo. Credit: Peter Sutherland.

bird will probably prefer you as its handler to anyone else. To avoid potential problems, try to introduce your bird to as many family members and friends as possible, as soon as the bird becomes tame. Let a friend offer your pet a treat to entice the bird on his arm. If your bird is timid, place the bird on the new person's arm or shoulder yourself. Then the bird will feel more assured and less frightened riding on the "stranger."

If no one but you ever handles the parrot, it may become totally devoted to you and become vicious to everyone else. This situation will include displays of "jealousy" if anyone shows familiarity to you. I had a parrot that would walk across rooms to bite a person sitting too close to me. A parrot that loves only you may not seem like a problem, but consider the consequences if your situation should change. For instance, who will care for your devoted pet if you take a vacation?

Birds, especially parrots, also have a tendency to react strongly to changes in your appearance. If you should suddenly appear at play time with newly-shampooed, wet hair; completely different clothing from when the bird just saw you; a radically different hair style or hair color; a new pair of glasses—your bird may not recognize you! If your pet is strongly attached to you, you may be surprised by its sudden rejection of you. It may take a few days for the bird to adjust to a significant change in your appearance. In rare cases, the bird may never adjust.

STAGE 6: TRAINING TO OBEY COMMANDS AND PERFORM TRICKS

A valuable bit of first training is to teach your bird to come to you on command. If your bird ever escapes to the outdoors, this lesson may help you get your pet back! You can teach this lesson regardless of whether your pet's wing is clipped. Call the bird to you with the command, "Roger (or whatever is your bird's name), *come!*" When the bird steps or lands on your arm, reward it with a tidbit. Be sure to say, "Come!" so the bird will associate the command, the desired action and the reward. While your pet is thoroughly learning this command, always provide a food reward. Later, you can substitute head scratching or another display of affection in the place of food.

A few people have been successful in "potty training" their parrots. In principle, this is a simple process of conditioning a bird to associate a word, an act and a place. In practice, this lesson requires months of training and patience. Naturally, mistakes are *never* punished!

"Potty training" is taught in two or three steps. First, you will need a relatively uncommon word as a command. Something like, "Gee whiz!" "Bingo!" or "Shazam!" will do. Choose a word and say it whenever you notice your pet performing the act. Do this for *at least* a month, so your bird will associate the word and the act thoroughly.

The "potty," of course, must be the bird's cage and play station(s). After the bird knows the meaning of your chosen command word, begin teaching it to associate the word and the act to a place. If you are holding your pet away from its play station and it performs, say the command word and carry it immediately to one of its "potties." When you arrive with the bird at the potty, say the word again. Continue to do this for at least another month. Then your bird will be able to make the necessary connections.

After the above is thoroughly learned, you can begin to take advantage of the training. When you go to pick up your pet to carry it away with you, give the command word before leaving the potty. The bird will probably perform, if necessary. Say, "Good bird!" to reinforce the behavior. Then, while you have your pet away from its cage or other potty, return to a potty with the bird every ten to fifteen minutes and repeat the command. You must provide opportunities to perform at reasonable time intervals to take advantage of your training effort.

Of course, if you prefer not to struggle with potty training, you can do the next best thing—prepare yourself. A bird that has the liberty of the house frequently selects a place to spend most of its time, with luck on its playground. However, this chosen place may be on a chandelier, a drapery pole, or the china cabinet. If so, a newspaper laid underneath this favored spot during the time the bird is out of the cage will eliminate most of the embarrassment you might experience. It is a simple thing to lay down the newspaper when you open the cage, then dump it when you close the door.

You can train almost any tame bird to perform simple tricks, as long as the tricks conform to the bird's physical abilities. For example, you cannot train a canary to carry a stick in its foot because this is beyond a canary's physical capabilities. A parrot, however, could perform this feat immediately.

Begin with simple "tricks" that correspond to your pet's natural abilities. Walking or hopping up a ladder is such a simple "trick." When the bird performs, give it a small tidbit as a reward. This will help your pet develop the ability to "learn."

After your pet can perform a few simple tricks and has figured out the reward system, try something more difficult. Ringing a bell for a treat is an example of a trick of intermediate difficulty. To teach your pet to perform this trick, try hanging a little bell on its play surface, say on the top of a ladder or swing. Then show the bird how to ring the bell a few times. When your pet rings the bell, hand it a treat. Keep doing this. Eventually, when your pet sees a treat, it will run up the ladder or jump on the swing and ring the bell to get it. Your bird may, in fact, perform its entire repertoire of tricks when it sees a treat!

By repeatedly showing your bird a trick and rewarding even a

In the following photographs "Frodo" Cigala demonstrates the training steps for learning to play dead. (Frodo is already a pro.) (1) Start with a tame subject and (2) accustom the bird to a hand on its back. Credit: Peter Sutherland.

3

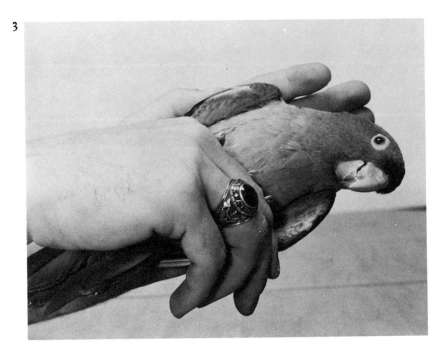

4

(3) *Gradually tip the bird to the side until* (4) *it rests on its back in your hand.*
Credit: Peter Sutherland.

5

(5) *Remove fingers.* Credit: Peter Sutherland.

partial performance, you can teach your pet more difficult tricks, like putting pennies in a bank or fetching. As long as your bird learns how to learn, through the reward method, you can train it to perform any number of tricks, limited only by your imagination and patience.

A hookbill or a mynah that likes to be petted and has confidence in its handler can learn to play "dead" or pretend it's sleeping very easily. The birds that learn these tricks usually enjoy the unusual positions. Basically, these tricks are taught over a period of weeks, by gradually increasing simple petting to holding your hand motionless over the bird's back. Then, as the bird gets used to this, you would begin to tip your hand over a little more every day until the bird is lying face-up in the palm of your hand. It helps to steady the bird if you let it hold your free fingers in its feet.

Once your bird will lie peacefully in your hand, you can try to teach it to stand on its head (actually the back of its head). To do this, lay the bird in your hand so that its head is face-up in the direction of your arm, its tail pointing toward your fingers. Then, gradually lift your fingers until the bird's body and tail are pointing straight upward while its head is still lying flat in your palm. After a few practice sessions, you can eventually straighten out your fingers so that the bird is standing on its head without your support. Of course, the bird will always need your support to get into this position.

Frodo stands on his head, by extension of the "playing dead" training. Credit:
Peter Sutherland.

CHAPTER 9

Training to Talk, Whistle or Sing

As with any other type of training, only repetition will teach your hookbill or mynah to whistle simple tunes or talk. Usually it is the trainer, not the bird, who is at fault if a bird does not learn. If you are going to try to train your bird, remember its short attention span, be consistent and, above all, be *patient*.

To train your bird to talk, start with a simple word like "Hello." Say it clearly over and over again in the same tone of voice, whenever you have a chance—when you're passing by the cage, when you give your bird a treat, and so forth. During a period of *low activity* in your bird's routine, take twenty minutes to repeat the word over and over. Schedule the lesson for the same time every day. Some people find it helpful to cover three sides of the bird cage to encourage the bird to concentrate on the lesson. Others consider this a distraction in itself. Eventually, your bird will attempt the word. Listen closely and continue to repeat the word often until the bird says the word clearly. A budgie or cockatiel will not speak as clearly as a large parrot, so keep this in mind.

Once your pet learns its first word, continue to use the word often so your bird will not forget it. Then go on to another word or short phrase, using the same approach. Try to choose words and phrases that will have meaning to you. This will make the bird's performance more enjoyable. Also, try to give subsequent voice lessons in more than one setting: in the cage, on the play surface, on your arm. If so, your bird will be less likely to associate "talking" with a place. This association may be the reason why some birds will talk only from a perch; others, only from your arm.

The first words are the most difficult to teach, but at some point, your bird will pick up new words and phrases at a faster rate. Until this point is reached, however, you might want to use a tape recorder or one of the many training records available to ensure the clarity of the voice and the perseverance and patience of the trainer.

If you use a tape recorder, don't waste your time or your wits repeating the same word over and over and over for twenty minutes. Buy an endless loop cassette. It will cost more than an ordinary blank cassette, but the advantages are well worth it. Endless loop cassettes usually have message capabilities ranging from ten to sixty seconds. The tape runs continuously until you shut off the tape recorder. Using one of these tapes, you can say your word, wait five or ten seconds, then say it again. That's all there is to it.

Occasionally, individual birds react negatively to speech training. If your bird seems to object to the monotony of training by behaving aggressively, try to reschedule the lesson for another period or stop the lessons completely for a few days. Then try again. If the bird resumes its aggressive behavior, quit. Your pet's tameness is far more valuable than its vocabulary.

Whistling. Following the same basic principles, you can teach some birds, particularly cockatiels and mynah birds, to whistle simple tunes. Bates and Busenbark, however, caution against teaching a mynah to whistle because they believe it inhibits the bird's ability to talk. So, if you want your mynah to talk, don't whistle to it at all. Simple whistles, like a wolf whistle, are picked up almost immediately. When your bird learns its first whistle, start another. You can teach the bird to whistle a short tune by teaching one bar at a time. Then gradually connect the bars into the complete song.

Singing. To get the greatest range out of your canary, play a record of singing canaries for your bird. The bird will sing along and pick up new singing patterns. This is exactly how your canary learned what it already knows how to sing—from other canaries!

CHAPTER 10

Miscellaneous Information

IF YOU FAIL TO TAME YOUR BIRD

Suppose you have done your very best over a respectable period of time and have failed to tame your bird. What else can you do? There are two basic alternatives: get help or replace the bird.

If you have made *any* progress with your pet, that is, you can now manage it easily outside the cage or you can feed it directly, enlisting outside help would be realistic. If the bird is particularly valuable (a rare or expensive species), outside help makes even more sense. Many petshops, particularly bird stores, offer a taming service. If you have access to such a service, pay the shop a visit to inspect the facilities and to discuss in detail your bird, your own taming attempt, their taming method and fees.

Other sources of potential help would include your local bird club members, bird breeders, or even an interested friend who might have just the special touch your pet requires. Your petshop owner or veterinarian may be able to suggest specific sources of help. Ask them. Consider professional animal trainers, too. Don't forget the periodicals listed in "Suggested Reading" as sources of information or places to advertise for help.

These same sources will help you place, sell or trade your bird, if desired, to an appropriate home. Your violet budgie may turn out to be exactly what a local breeder has been looking for. Your petshop owner may know someone who dreams of owning a Halfmoon Conure like yours. Your local zoo may be looking for a replacement for its deceased mynah bird. If you decide to dispose of your bird, spend the time necessary to find it the best possible new situation, and *be honest* about your reasons for selling. You will be showing your pet the final and ultimate kindness.

A SECOND PET?

If you have a satisfying relationship with your first pet bird, you may wonder whether to get a second. There are a few things you should be aware of. Generally speaking, birds appreciate the presence of other birds. They do not necessarily appreciate direct contact, however. So, if you decide to get a companion for your pet budgie, for example, understand that you cannot simply buy another budgie and add it to your pet's cage. You *must* get the new bird its own cage and introduce the birds gradually during their free time. Otherwise, one of your pets may suffer needless persecution or perhaps even starvation because of its jealous companion.

If the birds come to like one another, which is probable, your original relationship will change. If your motive for getting a second bird was to reduce the demands on your time made by the first, you may end up with two birds clamoring for your limited attention!

Obviously, a second cage and a gradual and cautious introduction are necessary if you add a bird of a different species to your household. If you have a lovebird and get another parrot-like bird, you'll have to watch out for the new bird's welfare, too. A lovebird is crazy enough to match beaks with a large macaw and would likely terrorize a gentle cockatiel. Large softbills and small hardbills or hookbills *never* mix. Your mynah might not eat your canary, but it will probably try—at least, from the canary's point of view.

If you are purchasing a mate for your pet, bear in mind the temperament of the birds in question. A Society Finch will not bother a prospective mate, but most other kinds of birds will and do. Even docile birds, like canaries, pigeons or doves, require an introduction through separate cage wires. Aggressive birds (i.e., hookbills, softbills and many finches) must be protected from each other and cautiously watched until harmony is obvious.

SHOULD YOU BREED YOUR PET BIRD?

The natural next step for someone who owns a tame, pet bird and tastes the pleasure and satisfaction of bird-keeping is to acquire more and different kinds of birds and even to attempt breeding. This is how my hobby developed, and I would not discourage anyone from taking a similar, but reasoned, plunge.

If you should develop the urge to breed birds, you may wonder whether to involve your pet. If your pet is tame, will it breed? Will its tameness diminish? The opinions of authorities on birds are divided on this issue. There really is no single answer to these questions. It depends on the birds involved as well as their mates. Success of the total venture depends on the background of the birds, too. For example, your handfed bird may breed freely, but it will not necessarily feed its chicks until maturity. Feeding seems to be an "imprinted" type of learning obtained in the nest. A bird that has had this learning interrupted unnaturally, like a handfed bird, is therefore never totally reliable.

In general, breeding birds become protective about their venture, reacting aggressively to outside interferences such as nest inspections. After an indeterminable number of such interferences, the birds may even abandon nest, eggs or chicks. The way your pet fits into this general scheme depends on it and its mate.

Assuming you have a well domesticated bird that is known as a free breeder (canaries, pigeons, budgies, lovebirds, etc., belong to this category), you will have the least worries. A tame canary or pigeon will probably breed successfully, regardless of the tameness of its mate or a normal amount of inquisitiveness on your part. However, the bird that is not used to your presence (your pet's untamed partner) may give up if you become too involved. Obviously, you will get nowhere without the complete cooperation of two birds. The tame bird of the pair will remain tame when the job is done.

With small hookbills, whose tameness is usually a degree greater than hardbills, the outcome of a breeding attempt is slightly less predictable. Most budgies and lovebirds, by the way, will not mate and breed unless they can see other birds of their kind doing the same thing. So, you would have to make a greater investment in birds and equipment to get your project started. If you pair a tame budgie with a "wild" mate, the wild bird might abandon operations if its mate is too friendly with you. Raising a family is serious business, so you can hardly blame a bird for not participating if its mate seems less than 100 percent involved! It is also possible that the wild bird might reject or bully your tame pet because it displays uncharacteristic behavior—friendship with a human. If so, failure is certain. Obviously, if the birds do breed, the tame party will be busy, so you should not encourage a show of affection or remove your pet from its mate for any reason. This would cause severe stress. In general, if you breed your pet, you should try to forget that it's a pet as long as it is breeding. Again, once the family is raised, there is no reason to expect your pet to become any less tame, based on my experience.

Larger hookbills are the least predictable. Many parrots show no interest in breeding before the age of five years or more. This should come as no surprise, considering the long life span of a parrot. Sexing parrots to determine a true pairing is also quite difficult. And, once parrots do breed, they usually become protective to the point of downright viciousness and will often abandon their efforts completely if disturbed. This is *not* the place to experiment in breeding if you are a beginner! I would not presume to predict the outcome of pairings, that is, tamed with tamed or tamed with untamed. You just can't tell. However, the first hybrid

This tame budgie peeks at its mate in the nestbox. A simple breeding setup.
Credit: Jean M. Hawthorne.

macaw bred in this country resulted from the breeding of a tame Scarlet Macaw mated to a tame Blue and Gold Macaw. These birds, I'm told, carried out a successful nesting operation and remained affectionate living-room pets during the entire job! This is contrary to what we expect from breeding macaws.

If you want to attempt breeding, any of the books listed in "Suggested Reading" at the end of this Handbook will describe the necessities: when the birds are in condition, when to start, cages, nests, feeding, incubation and expectations. If you consult a few sources before you get involved, you are more likely to succeed in your part of the venture. The rest is up to the birds.

IF YOUR PET ESCAPES

If your bird escapes to the outdoors, the chances of getting it back range from extremely poor to zero, so you should never relax any vigilance about screening windows or closing doors. If the bird does escape, two problems emerge immediately. First, the bird will not be familiar with the exterior of your home or your neighborhood, so even if it wants to come back, the bird will not recognize where to go. Second, a strong, high flyer, especially a heavily built parrot, will be able to cover a considerable distance within seconds. This aggravates the first problem.

Your best course of action is to keep your eye on the bird *constantly*. In a lucky (and rare) case, your bird may land in a nearby tree, realize it is lost, and remain there long enough for you to attempt retrieval. Some authors suggest bringing the bird's cage to the tree at this point in case the bird might be inclined to return to its home on its own.

My Severe Macaw once escaped. The bird's wing was clipped, but a few flight feathers had grown back, enabling the bird to fly. The bird was 100 yards away within seconds, before I could even focus on its direction! Fortunately, passers-by saw the bird land in a tree and pointed out its location. I was fortunate to enlist a helper to watch the bird while I ran for a ladder. As soon as I lifted the ladder against the tree, the bird flew to another tree. A friend then came to my aid and sprayed the tree and my bird thoroughly with a garden hose. Then, he climbed onto the tree (from a garage roof, risking his neck) to catch the bird. The bird flew off again but was so waterlogged, it fell to the ground. I caught it in a towel and took it home to dry. Needless to say, I learned my lesson!

Even in the lucky case, as outlined above, you really need help watching the bird at all times. You can then try to get more help. If you have had the foresight to train your bird to come to you on command, the training will really pay off. (The Berwick book listed in "Suggested Reading" gives excellent instructions on this training.) The key words are *help* and a large dose of *luck*.

If you lose your bird, someone may find it, so advertise in your news-papers, notify your local humane organization, and tell your local police. My mother took in a stray, tame budgie when it flew to her window. A friend of mine acquired a Halfmoon Conure the same way. They both checked the lost-and-found ads periodically with no success.

It may be no comfort to you, but even pampered pets appear to survive in wild conditions. There are whole colonies of budgies, for instance, existing in a wild state in California and the South. I've seen a flock of six to ten conures living in Brooklyn, New York, *during the winter.* I was told that these birds had frequented the neighborhood for years. There are many similar cases throughout the country.

The only practical solution for an escaped pet bird is *prevention.* Be careful.

PROBLEMS WITH THE TAME PET

"What can I do to stop my bird's biting?" I have to admit, I can't answer this question with any authority. I have a few suggestions, though. First, try to determine whether the varmint's bites are provoked. Does it nip you when you take it from its cage; when you offer it food; when you are just carrying the bird around? Put yourself in your bird's place and think about the situation(s). Reread Chapter 2 carefully. Are you en-couraging the bird to "mouth" by touching its beak? If your bird wants to play this way, hand it a chew toy when it nips. (Never give it an obvious reward like food!) Think about the bird's routine. Are you bothering your pet when it's not in the mood? Is the biting accompanied by other displays of aggression, typical of breeding desires? If you can think of a reason for your bird's behavior, you are more than halfway down the road to curing it. Just try to eliminate whatever it is that your bird objects to. If you can't eliminate it, try to work around it. If you can't work around it, be patient and try not to overrate the seriousness of the problem.

If you think your pet's attacks are unprovoked, do your best to handle the situation calmly as it occurs. It is a serious mistake to display fear or panic to a bird. Somehow, they sense it and almost always get the better of you. I realize that it's difficult to act nonchalant about a bird bite—I'm not very good at it. A bird that develops the habit of biting becomes harder and harder to love.

Perhaps the best course of action with the unprovoked biter is to make sure that the bird is *never,* in any way, shape or form, rewarded for this behavior. I do not mean to imply that you should try to punish the bird. I mean that you should not develop a consistent reaction to the bites that the bird might consider a reward of sorts. For example, if you put the bird down immediately after biting (because you don't want to carry the little ingrate), a bite may come to mean, "Put me down! *Now!*" Once your bird develops such an effective line of communication, you will have an even bigger problem.

"How do I peel this critter off my shoulder?" This is a "nicer" problem than biting but can become very annoying. There's a simple answer: Use bird sense! Dump the bird by bending down near your bird's cage or play station, then nudge it on. Like your spirits, the bird would rather be high than low. Keep the bird's nails trimmed, too, so you won't be too uncomfortable when the bird is being so clingy. I remember many a summer when there were "bird tracks" all over my arms and shoulders! If the bird doesn't want to go home, reread the suggestions for returning a tame pet to its cage in Chapter 8 (Stage 2). Maybe an adjustment to its freedom time (more time, less time or a return to a *scheduled* time) would help. Of course, if you have an appointment an hour from now, don't take your bird out of its cage at all.

"The neighbors are getting up a petition to have me evicted! What can I do to stop my bird's screaming?" It is almost impossible to stop a bird's screaming once it starts, but you can at least try to reduce it. I suggest you consider the problem, like biting, from the bird's point of view. Does anything in particular provoke the noise? Turning on a radio? Your arrival home? Your departure? If so, try to work around the problem. Maybe you're not paying enough attention to your pet. Maybe your bird is so happy, it wants to tell the world!

There is only one "solution" to screaming I know of, and it is to cover the bird as soon as it starts. This is not exactly punishment; you could call it negative reinforcement. I am not completely convinced that this treatment is humane, though. Birds are supposed to make noise and it is unfair to keep them silent. Consider the case of a barking dog. Senseless barking is usually discouraged; but barking to announce an intruder is good and should be rewarded. Barking has its place. So, too, does the bird's noise-making.

Suggested Reading

Following are lists of books and periodicals you will want to investigate for further information. The book list is by no means exhaustive; there are many other titles available. However, in terms of quality of information and coverage of bird species, the list is complete, reliable and excellent. Books marked "British orientation" provide sometimes markedly different diets for birds than recommended in this book. The reason for this is the varying availability of foodstuffs.

A well stocked petshop will carry some of these books. Your local library may also have copies or be able to borrow them from other libraries in the system. The addresses of lesser-known publishers are provided in the book list. Otherwise, there are two good mail-order sources of bird books:

Avian Publications, 310 Maria Drive, Wausau, WI 54401.
Audubon Publishing Co., 3449 North Western Avenue, Chicago, IL 60618.

The periodicals provide an ongoing source of information about cage and aviary birds of particular interest to breeders. Pet bird topics are also featured, and many contributing columnists answer questions from readers in a portion of every column. Unfortunately, there is sometimes misinformation in a few articles. Well-meaning authors occasionally perpetuate myths, suggest unhealthy folk remedies for serious conditions, and so on, under what seems to be but is not the aegis of the magazine's editors. You must be able to separate the wheat from the chaff, so to speak, to benefit from the information.

BOOKS

On Species Characteristics and Care

Bates, Henry J. and Robert L. Busenbark. *Parrots and Related Birds.* Neptune City, NJ: T.F.H. Publications, 1969.
This book provides complete information on parrots and parrot-like birds, including a chapter on taming. This is the second edition of a highly regarded classic. It is still one of the best. Clothbound.

————. *Finches and Soft-Billed Birds*. Neptune City, NJ: T.F.H. Publications, 1970.
This book covers finches, doves, quail, and softbilled birds. Also a classic, it is the best available. Clothbound.

————. *Guide to Mynahs*. Neptune City, NJ: T.F.H. Publications, 1966.
The best available book on all kinds of mynahs, it is a must for every mynah bird owner. Paperback.

Clear, Val. *Common Cagebirds in America*. New York: Bobbs-Merrill, 1966.
As the title suggests, this book features the popular varieties of cagebirds. The author is a well known authority on birds and a talented writer; as a result, the book is not only complete, it is pleasant reading as well. A good, basic reference. Paperback.

Forshaw, Joseph M. *Parrots of the World*. New York: Doubleday, 1977. Also available now in a less expensive reprint edition through T.F.H. Publications, this book provides field information and breeding notes on every known species of parrot. Very well illustrated. Clothbound.

Freud, Arthur. *All About the Parrots*. New York: Howell Book House, 1980.
Although devoted primarily to the larger hookbills, this book also covers conures, cockatiels, budgies and other species. It provides many insightful and unique hints on the care of pet birds as well as other highly useful information. Not just another parrot book. Clothbound.

Lafeber, T.J., D.V.M. *Tender Loving Care for Pet Birds*. 1977: Dorothy Products, 818 S. Seminary, Park Ridge, IL 60068.
A useful little book explaining in clear language the body systems of a bird and the danger signals of disease, it also contains many tips on how to make your pet happier. A worthy addition to your bird book library. Paperback.

Low, Rosemary. *Parrots of South America*. London: John Gifford, 1972. Low provides complete information on South and Central American hookbills, including macaws, conures, parakeets and parrotlets, small parrots and Amazons. Every aspect of care and breeding is discussed. British orientation. Clothbound.

Naether, Carl A. *Raising Doves and Pigeons: An Introduction to Their Behavior and Breeding*. New York: David McKay, 1979.

A very good, basic book on pigeons and doves, providing insight into their unique behavior. The book also offers instructions on training Racing Homers, Rollers and Tipplers. Popular doves and a few foreign pigeons are covered. Clothbound.

————. *The Book of the Pigeon and of Wild Foreign Doves.* Fifth Edition. New York: David McKay, 1964.
Originally published in 1939, this updated version covers all kinds of domestic pigeons and foreign doves as well as their care and breeding. It is well illustrated. Clothbound.

Rogers, Cyril H. *Encyclopedia of Cage and Aviary Birds.* (Val Clear, Advisory Editor.) New York: Macmillan, 1975.
In this complete reference book, Rogers covers birds alphabetically within seven broad groups (canaries, budgerigars, zebra finches and Bengalese, parakeets, parrots and allied species, aviary-bred British birds and exotic birds). Housing, feeding and breeding information is provided for each group. British orientation softened by Val Clear. Clothbound.

Rutgers, A. *The Handbook of Foreign Birds in Colour. Volumes 1 and 2.* London: Blandford Press, 1964.
Volume 1 of this work covers finches and softbills. Volume 2 describes quail, partridges, pheasants; pigeons and doves; waterfowl; and parrot-like birds. Both volumes provide complete care, feeding and breeding data and are well illustrated. British orientation. Clothbound.

On Training

Beckmann, Ed. *Love, Praise & Reward: The New Way to Teach Your Dog.* New York: Coward, McCann & Geoghegan, 1979.
This is obviously not a bird book, but the concepts presented are highly useful to anyone serious about training. Chapter 3, "Understanding Your Dog's Mind," could easily be renamed "Understanding Your Bird's Mind." Regardless of your training intentions, this book is valuable reading for anyone with a pet, furred or feathered. Clothbound.

Berwick, Ray. *How to Train Your Pet Like a Television Star.* Los Angeles: Armstrong Publishing, 1977.
Written by the leading bird and animal trainer in both the television and motion picture industries, this book reveals how he does it. Every step is illustrated. Fred, the cockatoo co-star of the *Baretta* television series, is featured. Dog, cat and other animal training programs are also included. Paperback.

Kalvan, Jay and Hazel. "Housebreaking a Parrot!" *American Cage-Bird Magazine*. Volume 47, No. 9, September 1975, p. 19.
This is the source of the "potty training" instructions outlined within.

PERIODICALS

American Cage-Bird Magazine. 3449-51 North Western Avenue, Chicago, IL 60618.
Published monthly. Features articles of interest to cage-bird owners and breeders, club directory and show dates. Contains more classified advertising than any other bird magazine.

American Pigeon Journal. P.O. Box 278, Warrenton, MO 63383.
Published monthly. Devoted to all branches of pigeon raising—fancy, utility and racing. Includes a column by Dr. John T. Ervin, a veterinarian who specializes in pigeons, providing excellent advice to readers on pigeon problems. Furnishes club information, show dates and plenty of advertising.

Bird World. P.O. Box 70, North Hollywood, CA 91603.
Published bi-monthly. Features articles on canaries, parrots, doves and other cage birds of interest to breeders and pet owners. Includes a question-and-answer column by an avian medicine specialist, Dr. Raymond A. Kray, D.V.M. Clubs, show dates and advertising are also included.

Feather Fancier. R.R. 5, Forest, Ontario, Canada N0N 1J0.
A monthly newspaper for Canadian fanciers of standard-bred poultry, fancy pigeons, racing pigeons and pet stock.

Gazette. 1155 East 4780 South, Salt Lake City, UT 84117.
Published nine times a year. A magazine for game bird breeders, aviculturalists, zoologists and conservationists, it features articles of interest to fanciers of pheasants, foreign doves, quail, waterfowl, peafowl and others. Advertising includes exotic animals and breeding parrots.

Watchbird. P.O. Box 327, El Cajon, CA 92020.
Magazine published bi-monthly by the American Federation of Aviculture. Features articles of interest to breeders of cage and aviary birds, reports on restrictive legislation, show dates and advertising. Subscription to *Watchbird* includes membership in the American Federation of Aviculture.

Index

Page numbers in **boldface** indicate photographs.
C.Pl. denotes color plate.